THE BELLY
OF A
WOMAN

Poetic Truths of an Extraordinary Journey

SHANET DENNIS

THE BELLY OF A WOMAN

Poetic Truths of an Extraordinary Journey

Copyright © 2008 by Shanet Dennis

ISBN 978-0-578-00269-9

This book is dedicated to my husband Christopher Dennis for allowing me the freedom to simply be myself and constantly reminding me that it is okay to remember my past. I thank God for sending me a partner who is not selfish, but comfortable enough with himself to share me with all of you.

I am absolutely in love with loving you!

Acknowledgments

The completion of this little book has been a long time coming. It could not exist without the many people who encouraged me along the way. I want to thank my mother. I don't think you realize it, but you are my most cherished and greatest inspiration. To all of my family, thanks for making me feel like I was somebody special all of my life. Thanks to Seitress for listening to my poems, and giving me praise and criticism. If it wasn't for you fixing my cheap little computer, this project may still be collecting dust on my zip drive. To all of my girlfriends, Parisha, Serena, Latrice, Donni, Contessa, Sherrie and all who I forget to name, thank you for always asking me to recite my poetry. Because of you, I believed my work was worth something. To the many people who inspired my works, thank you, thank you, thank you for giving me something juicy to write about. Special thanks to Iyanla Vanzant, Mya Anglou, Nicki Giovonni and Sista Soulja. Because of you and your works I have the courage to tell my own story.

Foreword

I would first like to say this book is about personal, feminine, and spiritual growth. I've done things I've been proud and ashamed of, and I have carried the shameful things deep in my belly. But just as a baby develops in the womb, there comes a time when that pregnancy can no longer be hidden and a birth must take place. After adding piles and piles of undesirable junk into my belly, it had finally gotten to the point where I could no longer bare the weight of carrying it all. I could no longer hide it. I had to release. So I began to share some of my hardships with other women. I had no idea that so many of us had similar stories. After talking, crying, and praying together, we found that we needed each other. I wished that we would talk more often, but I understood that feeling of not wanting to be judged by our pasts. I also realized that sharing helps to accelerate the healing process. We can truly learn from one another's experiences. So I give you this book full of love, pain, joy, tears, laughter, loneliness, fear, desperation, happiness, shame, and the supreme feeling of accomplishment in hopes that through these simple words we learn to let go together.

Contents

THE BELLY
OF A
WOMAN

MILESTONE

Love, live, breathe...life!

Breathe

If we hold our breath too long we die.

Stop putting your dreams and aspirations on hold.

"Waiting" or "holding your breath" only leads to one thing.

Love yourself enough to know that you can do whatever your mind and heart can fathom right now!

You don't have to wait.

With everything that God has given you...

BREATHE!

Doesn't it feel good?

Live Life!

My life is meant to be lived
in its completeness.
I thank God that within my meekness
lies the ability to know what I want
and go after it fearlessly.
Clearly understanding that tomorrow is not promised
and today is a gift…
I am readily willing to take the risk.
Knowing that healthy things grow
and growing things change
and change is inevitable…
Trying to prolong it is only regrettable.
But not everyone is as blessed.
As I enjoy life so much more
yet require so much less to do so.
I'm thankful that I know what makes me happy
this makes me so much stronger
Because for so many others it takes so much longer
Taking the straight and narrow
to simply eliminate doubt
Or spending their entire lives trying figure it out!
FREEDOM!
Some say my life's decisions are unorthodox.
But who can be free trapped inside of a box
that society has built for those who
choose not to pave their own way.
Giving them step by step instruction on
"How to secure tomorrow today"
No thank you!
I choose to be secure today

Be sure today that my life is filled.
Not drilled in monotony
I've got to be thrilled with each new day
so when my time finally comes I am able to say...
I LIVED LIFE!

Elucidation

Sometimes I did things just because it made me feel good. I just wanted to smile since smiling is an outward expression of what's going on inside. I would get up in the morning and decide that I didn't want to go to work. I felt that I would much rather go for a walk, have breakfast, and do some writing. Needless to say, that's exactly what I did on most occasions. I made those types of spontaneous decisions often because I watched the people around me float through life with frowns on their faces. They were working dead end jobs or just dealing with a whole bunch of STUFF. I didn't want that to be me. I know that as women we naturally deal with ups and downs in life, but what we don't realize is that a lot of it has to do with the choices we make. We can change the things that bring us down almost instantaneously.

The joy I found when I learned I had the power of choice is something I cherish with my whole being. When I learned that I was happier doing the things that catered to my needs and not what society expected of me, I grew into someone I could love. I was confident and secure in any environment. I found out who I was and was able to share that with the people around me. So I say to my peers: Live Life! Do it for yourself. Not for your mother, father, teacher, husband, boyfriend, children, the world. Don't live up to everybody else's expectations. Create your own and exceed them.

Dear Mama

I remember a time
when all I felt was pain
and most of my happy moments
were shadowed by my shame
No contentment.
All I felt was resentment.
I cried because I needed you
Was mad because you needed to do
whatever it was that kept you away.
Just trying to live was a struggle every day.
Striving to find my place in this world
feeling like a motherless girl.
When I came into womanhood alone
I prayed that God would send you home.
Blindly guided by my peers
I was living far beyond my years,
because of this section in my life
when I did not have your direction.
Didn't have your advice.
I placed myself in harmful situations.
Was raped at thirteen in a desert location.
Molested twice a few years before that.
I never said a word.
I carried the weight on my back.
Smoked my first joint at eleven.
Smoked 25 to be exact
I didn't know what I was doing
so my high came from the contact.
But God did send me an angel
to keep me out of trouble

she came and shared my music with me
and help keep my spirit at its highest level
instead of roaming the streets at night
or letting some man lay me down.
I spent my time writing music
and being creative with my sound.
You don't realize how this kept me
God came down and gave me a gift
and because he knew I was so lonely
he gave me someone to share it with
Someone who shared my same struggles,
for her mother was lost too
So God gave us to each other
To help us make it through
But when he brought you back to me
you could do no good in my sight
when I thought about all that went wrong
there was nothing you could do to make it right.
for a long time I rebelled
I wanted you to pay
for every minute, every hour
every day you spent away.
but then I had a child of my own
and did all I was able to do.
and that's when I finally realized
that you did all that you could too!
and I appreciate every moment
that I am able to share with you now
all the life lessons
all the answered questions
because you are able to show me how
to be a strong mother, a strong women,

You've shown me how to overcome
regardless of the circumstance
every battle can be won!

Elucidation

Every time I read this it makes me cry. Sometimes it hurts to remember. I wrote this piece for my mother because there were things I had never told her. Things she needed to know before our time together was up. My mother was sick. I don't know how long she was on drugs, but I know her addiction started taking its toll when I was about eleven years old. I could see things around us changing. The house wasn't as clean as it usually was. I started seeing more and more strange faces coming and going with little or no introduction. I soon lost the desire to be home. I wanted to be anywhere my mother was not. I didn't have the option of living with my father because not only did I not know him, I didn't know where he was. By the time I had turned thirteen, we were evicted from our apartment and moved in with my aunt Sheryl. I was happier there. I had freedom to hang with friends and just be a normal teenager. At least it felt that way until I would be at a local burger stand with friends and they'd ask "Is that your mama over there clucked out? I didn't know your mama was a clucker." That was the term used at the time for a person addicted to crack. I remember being so embarrassed. I got used to it over time though. I became comfortable with the idea that I didn't have a mother to go home to. Didn't have a mother to cook my meals or talk to me about the way my body was changing. I finally had to face and accept the new reality of my life.

I started putting myself in compromising situations. I went to weekly house parties that were given by local gangsters. We were sure to be in a shoot-out at every event. But that didn't keep me away. This is what I did to cope. I started paying attention to the things I could gain from men. There was one man in particular who knew how to woo me. He was my best friend's cousin and was also a drug dealer. He often told me how cute I was and offered me money to ride here and there with him. Being naïve, I obliged. After multiple dealings of this nature, I knew what to expect. A hug or maybe a kiss on the cheek is all he had asked for. One night he asked me to ride with him and I jumped in his car gladly. He drove me to the Long Beach shipyard (which was abandoned at the time) and made his way into my pants. I was nervous and on my period. He didn't care. There was no one around so I didn't want to make a wrong move. I let him go as far as trying to stick his penis inside me, but it hurt so bad I told him to stop. He pushed harder. I told him to stop again. He didn't stop. This is when I looked around me and realized I was being raped. I could hear him mumbling things like "You got me hard out here and you wanna tease me? I'm getting this ass tonight." I just started screaming and finally he stopped, pulled his pants up and drove me to his house. I remember being in shock and thinking "Is Tee really going to rape me?" He was. He did. I went straight to the bathroom and got cleaned up. When I came out he had all these new clothes lying around and told me to pick what I wanted. I grabbed a few things and he took me home.

There was a lot of getting high and drinking Boones Farm. This made me feel grown, popular, and accepted by my peers. I was known for being able to roll joints the best because I learned how from watching my mother. But over time I grew tired of being the "bad girl." I wanted to do something positive and I found a voice. I found my voice. I started to sing in talent shows at school, and the more people told me I had a nice voice the more I believed it. This became my outlet. It wasn't long before I met Kelly and learned that we had this gift in common. We grew closer because of music and the fact that both of our mothers at the time were addicts. I finally felt like I had someone to relate to. Someone who truly understood my struggle. I had had enough sympathy from everyone around me. After being numb for so long, God gave me something that made me feel again: music and Kelly. Because of these two tangible elements my struggles didn't seem as bad. This is what carried me through.

My mother finally got it together. It took three years for her to beat the addiction. She got us a new apartment and we started a new, drug-free life. It felt so good to be home. To be back in the care of my mama. But it wasn't long before I grew angry. I was mad with my mother for leaving me alone during those formative years. I was angry because I had to see her on the streets and have her ask me for money at thirteen. I wanted to know what took her so long to come back. But I couldn't ask those questions. I don't know why I couldn't. But I just could not. She was so happy. She was healthy and doing so well. I guess I just didn't want to be the one to remind her of the pain. So instead, I chose to rebel. If she said up, I said down. If she said stay, I went. I wanted it to be hard for her because I felt like she made it hard for me. It was a struggle, but I did gain clarity. When I got pregnant at seventeen, my mother catered to my every need in ways that I had never witnessed. She gave me what only a mother could give. She cared when I was sick. It mattered to her if I had eaten or not. It was those little things; the priceless things that triggered my epiphany. This is when I realized that my mother was really giving me her all and I couldn't ask for anything more. I learned to appreciate her and I thanked God for sending her back to me. I knew so many others whose mothers are still lost to this addiction. But my mother...my Mama is a fighter. Her strength and will is admirable, and it taught me that no matter the level of adversity, I will overcome.

Mama, I love you.

My Best Friend Didn't Tell Me

I was a spunky nineteen-year old girl in the prime of her life. At least, that's what I thought. I was single and good looking. I had gotten pregnant by a high school class mate. Though we had fun, that relationship didn't last six months. My daughter was now about four months old. Well, let me start from the beginning. My best friend Kelly and I were as tight as a rock. We did almost everything together. We were roommates, classmates, band mates, and whatever else a person can think of. We would tell people who didn't know us that we were sisters. Although we may not have been blood sisters, she was definitely my God-sent sister. We were as close as any family member could be, if not closer. She had a cousin named Bobby. He was her cousin by marriage. So, of course, he was my cousin too. I met him when I was about sixteen. He would come over and hang out with us. We would eat burgers, pizza, and smoke marijuana. He would be the one telling us we shouldn't be doing that type of stuff. The big brother with some sense that neither one of us had.

We went on like that for some years. One day, after not seeing Bobby for a while, he came over with his new girlfriend. She was beautiful. He seemed happy so we were happy for him. It wasn't long after that until he started showing up at our house a little more frequently than normal. He had a new car, a new job, and seemed to be doing quite well for a black, nineteen-year-old man on the straight and narrow. It was summer of August 1997 when he asked me if I knew how to drive a stick shift. I didn't know how to drive at all! He said, "Let's go!" I was so excited that I hurried to the car without even asking Kelly to keep and eye on Miracle (my daughter) for me. Bobby was a good teacher. He asked a lot of questions about my date life and my daughter's father. I was so clueless that I spilled the beans about everything. A day or two later, Kelly comes into my bedroom to tell me that Bobby called and told her he likes me and he wanted to know if it would be okay with her if we dated. I was shocked and surprised that he would try to be a gentleman about it. She gave me his number and I called him that evening.

Now I was already dating this guy named Robert who I really enjoyed but I *knew* Bobby. He was my friend. That meant something to me. I dated them both for a while until that whole situation became too taxing. I had to choose and I chose Bobby. My birthday was coming up and I had a party planned that I had already invited Robert to. I explained this to Bobby and he was comfortable with me keeping my plans as they were. He didn't show up at the party. I know…How thoughtful, right? I spent my last evening with Robert and was now able to focus completely on Bobby. We had fun. I did things I hadn't done before with anyone and it felt good. It wasn't long before we began to have our ups and downs and I noticed that he and Kelly weren't getting along too well. They were arguing and cursing each other out. They were snapping at each other like they weren't family. She would tell me to talk to him but I didn't want to get involved. I felt like that was their family business and I wanted them to handle it. So I stayed neutral throughout that whole ordeal. It became harder and harder to listen to both of them bicker so I made arrangements to move out.

I stayed with my grandmother for a couple of months to save money before my daughter and I moved into a one-bedroom apartment on the east side of Long Beach. That's when the problems between Bobby and I became more prevalent. He would show up at my door at all hours of the night. He didn't want to contribute to my household yet he wanted to be there every day. I became pregnant twice but our relationship was so rocky that I made the decision to abort both babies. I just couldn't see myself raising another child alone. It was only a matter of months before we had "The Talk." We were lying in bed together when he said that he had something to tell me. He explained that he didn't want to have any secrets between us. I agreed and patiently waited for him to continue. The tension in the air was thick for the split second of silence before he said, "I slept with Kelly." It took a minute for me to digest what he was telling me. After confirming whether or not he was serious, I asked all of the who's, what, when, where's, and why's. He told me that it happened almost two years earlier before she and I were roommates. This confused me. I didn't understand why he was telling me this now. He told me that he wasn't sure if I had known or not. Well, I didn't. I had absolutely no idea. After all, they were family. I called Kelly in that very moment to ask her if it was true. She confirmed it and abruptly said she didn't want to talk about it; it was in the past and she didn't know why he would tell me that. The only question I had at the time was "Why in the hell didn't you tell me?"

A day or two, or weeks, went by before we spoke. We didn't call. Put in our best efforts to avoid each other. At least I did. I was disappointed because we lived by the unspoken rule that if any one of us girlfriends went out with, had interest in, or slept with a guy, he was off limits to the rest of us. Had I known they were intimate I would have never gone there and even if I wanted to…they took away my power to choose. Before I was involved they spoke about it and made a decision without me. Bobby and I spoke about it in detail I'd rather not explain. We parted ways soon after.

Kelly finally called but it was to make an appointment to get her hair braided. Even with all of the built-up animosity, I agreed. When she arrived we didn't say much. Conversation couldn't have been more forced. Her cousin Tara and sister Sharon came by while she was there. They fell into the usual girl talk and it wasn't long before Kelly started sending subliminal messages. I can't remember her exact words, but she mentioned people speaking up on stuff that is irrelevant to them. That was followed by people minding their own business not mentioning her name. I got the point. She made it clear that she didn't want me to bring up what had happened so I chose to cater to her comfort.

It took a while but we did get back to normal. However, I couldn't trust her. She would normally be the person I came to when I needed to talk about things like this. I didn't want to make it seem like I was gossiping about her, so for a long time I didn't tell anyone. I asked myself if I could still befriend someone whom I felt betrayed me. Over time, I swept it under the rug just as she did, so I guess one would say that I could. But Kelly and I were never the same after that. I was never the same after that. I questioned the integrity of my other girlfriends. I felt that if the person I trusted most would leave out such a minor yet major detail, why wouldn't anyone else? Eventually I matured enough to somewhat empathize.

MILESTONE

Give.

Then when you feel like you have given all you have...

Give some more

I Cried

My own version of Iyanla Vanzant's "Yesterday I Cried"

I'm crying
A sorrowful cry I'm crying
Because I feel a huge portion
Of my insides are dying
I'm weeping over all the things
I said I'd do, but did not
And all the promises I made to myself and others
And honestly forgot
I'm sniffling over situations I chose to be in
But never made a choice
I'm crying because inside I was screaming
So no one could hear my voice
I'm hurting because not every hand dealt to me
Was a hand I dealt myself
I'm tired of giving everyone 100%
And when I'm in need I have nothing left
I'm praying to God for guidance and strength
Because I know he's never too late
Then I'm finding myself down in tears again
Because I didn't have the patience to wait
I'm crying because things in my life seems so right
And yet other things still seem so wrong
I'm walking this road and tears still seems to flow
Cause I feel its just taking too long
I'm crying because my emotions are slowly
Chipping my insides away
So I'm here on my knees, its just two after three

Barely making it through the day
So I'm crying
I'm crying a humble cry
I'm crying in search of liberation
With no form of hesitation
I'm crying, I'm crying, I'm crying

I cried
Yesterday I cried
And oooh it felt so good to me
Like the chill of a breeze on a summer's eve
Reading a book under a backyard tree
I cried so good I looked like an old grey woman
With big puffy bags under her eyes
But I really didn't mind
Because at the end of my cry
Like an old woman I was nothing but wise
Yesterday I cried for so long
That I thought I'd be weak but was surprisingly strong
I called up some friends I hadn't heard from in years
To tell them the story of my spirit filled tears
Then I popped in my gospel, drew me a bath, and poured
myself some wine
Had my Lord there with me, my aromatherapy
And was feeling nothing but fine
I cried, I cried
Yesterday I cried
And I'm so glad I did it yesterday
Because it feels good to know
That when I'm on the go
My hurt has been swept away
After my cry when I lifted my eyes

I went to work and did my job with my head held high
I laughed, I sang, I did everything
And no one knew from where my sudden joy came
That night I played with my daughter
And rocked her to sleep
Then I kissed and massaged her crooked little feet
Oh yes, Yesterday I cried
I cried a humble cry
I cried in search of liberation
A spiritual conversation
Now I'm happy with my situation
Because I'm crying, I'm trying, I'm striving.

Elucidation

Iyanla Vanzant wrote a poem called "Yesterday I Cried". This poem spoke to me because I could relate with where it came from. I needed to cry a similar type of cry. I needed to hear it during a time when I felt like all I could do was scream to gain any type of release and I thank God for her gift. I'm so happy she was able to share it with me. Iyanla is one of my many inspirations for choosing to tell my own story. I respect her as a person, a woman, a mother, and a writer.

Thank you, Iyanla, for "Yesterday I Cried."

The Busy Woman

I work all day
Standing on my feet
Some days go by when I'm too tired to eat
At times I get the feeling that my battle's never won
Because when I get home from a hard day's work
My work is still not done
I have to cook
I must clean
I have to laugh
I have to sing
Because my baby girl is only two
She doesn't know what the day has put me through
I have to talk
I have to read
I have to draw
I have to play
And after all my work is done
I have to take time out to pray
Now day is gone
Night has come
And dawn is yet to be
And I'm fatigued at the fact
That there is no time left for me.
Now I'm crying
Because I'm tired
I can't express this any other way
And I still need time to rest
In preparation for the following day
I'm a woman
A busy woman

I'm a woman with many needs
And I can't fulfill them all alone
Can somebody help me please?
I do what I do
In one day not two
Because on the second day I must repeat the first again
And in the process
I have to deal with immature men.
Come on you guys!
Give me a break
You're suppose to be helping me for God's sake
I mean,
It's really a hindrance in my day
When the first word in your conversation is "Hey"
Then when you notice you were extremely rude
You want to stroke and massage my attitude
By constantly complimenting my slender sleek physique
Yes!
 I feel that's a sign of your conversational weakness
And I can't deal with this everyday
You guys are making it hard
Cause I don't have the kind of time in my day
To be holding up my guard
I'm already holding my tongue
Holding onto faith
 I'm holding my daughter too
And some of you have the nerve to think
I'm supposed to be holding you!
Wanting me to pick you up
Pay half on a date
But brother, I didn't order nothing on your plate
Now,
I know some of you might have a lowered chest

Cause I touched on you and your financial weakness.
But see, I don't have time
For this kind of burden in my life
I'm at the point where I'm doing too good
To be welcoming in strife.
Cause I'm a woman
A busy woman
I'm a woman with many needs
But I can't fulfill them all alone
Can somebody help me please?
I'm well taken care of
And very much in love with myself
But once again you must understand
That a sister needs some help.
Stop by my job and treat me to lunch
When my daughter says she's thirsty
Run to the store to buy her some punch.
When you see me washing dishes
Come over and help me rinse.
The kind of help I need from a man
Is really common sense.
Before I run to get my toddler from the sitter
Take me home and run me a bath.
When you see that the day has made me bitter
Sing me a song that will make me laugh
I need help from a man
Who is going to challenge me
Someone with a loving, spiritual mentality
Someone fit to sit next to this Queen on her throne
Cause I'm a busy woman with many needs
And I can't fulfill them all alone.

Can somebody help me please?

Elucidation

I laugh when I read this piece. I was so upset. I had just turned twenty years old. I was single and carrying the weight of a single parent on my shoulders. I was a hair stylist at a salon called S-Touch so I was always tired from working long hours. I'm sure all of you young working single mothers can relate. My daughter was so demanding at that time. She was intelligent and expressed her needs clearly. Me being the only other person in the house, I had to entertain. During this period in my life I needed some attention. I wanted someone to cater to my needs the way I had to cater to my baby's. To all the men reading this…the little things really do make a difference. I simply wanted some help which I thoroughly expressed throughout this entire piece. Every time I left my house I was bombarded by men with their pants hanging from the bottom of their butts who expected me to entertain the idea of exchanging contact information. It drove me nuts. I just wanted to meet a normal man with sense enough to wear their pants the right way and use proper English. Was that too much to ask for? I didn't think so. So, to all you young sisters out there doing it all by yourself, I understand your struggle. Stay strong cause help is on the way. It may not come in a talk dark and handsome package right away, but stay patient and it will be right on time.

MILESTONE

Love everything you do...
And you won't have to work a day in your life!

Path of My Pen

My joy and solace is found in my pen
Experiences
Only a woman can truly know
Only my sisters can empathize
Journeys
Most choose not to share with others
Shame
Feeling like we're the only one
Passion
Felt by the young, single and married
Overwhelming sensations
of love lost, gained, and hard to maintain
Motherhood
the courage it takes to say…I'm doing my best
when others think the opposite
Gratitude
to thank our own mothers for giving us
all they had to give
Self love
Knowing when to say your time in my life
Has come and gone,
but thank you for the lessons
My pen is my remedy
My pen is how I say…listen
My pen is there when I need to
share my experiences
and all of my lessons
with those who need to read it
Need to hear it
My pen is there when God tells me to Write!

Elucidation

This is my answer to all the questions why? People wonder why I chose to tell my story as if I'm doing something that's taboo. I'm led to believe this is because of the vast differences in the content of my work. What they fail to understand is that people grow and change. I have experiences as a young woman searching to find self. So I write about that. I have experiences as a young single mother. So I write about that. I have experiences as a woman searching to find spirituality. I write. I was a woman who was heartbroken. I write. I was a woman in love. I write. I was woman in lust. I write. I was betrayed. I write. This is the path of my pen. My journey through life in truth. My hope is that I touch and encourage someone else in the same manner that so many others have touched me.

My Ghetto

In my ghetto
The children wear socks with no elastic
And...
Patent leather jackets that's really plastic
And...
Their idea of a joke is being sarcastic
And...
Their mothers are young
Ghetto sprung
So they know no better.
In my ghetto
Some people call it fabulous!
And sometimes I get mad at this
Because the streets are cracked
And filled with black drippings
And my baby can't skate across the street without tripping
And nobody's stressing the point
So the power of our voice is slipping.
In this ghetto of mines
We're having real hard times
Dealing with hate crimes
And we can't call one-time
Cause they're the ones doing all the hating
The blue collar Klan has got our young brothers shaken
And some brothers retaliating
But can you blame them?
Of course.
So you shame them in courts.
In my ghetto
Our elders are speaking

But they're not reaching are youth
Because they're keeping the truth
About their past lives locked down
And then they cock frowns at the thought
of history repeating itself.
In my ghetto
Chivalry isn't dead
If your man makes your bed after you lay down
But then you dread him leaving you
If you don't stay down
So what's the point in that?
You can't reach a goal lying on your back.
The Ghetto
My Ghetto
Some people call it fabulous!
And some times I get mad at this
Because people are dying
The Government's lying
Preachers are trying
And babies are crying for attention
Mothers are lazy
The system is crazy
And the vision of our future is hazy
Our music is hurting
Excuses aren't working
Brothers are flipping
And sisters are tripping
So…
Can we get a grip on the jungle fever?
And the…
I would leave her…
But she might file child support.

All this happens in my Ghetto
And I haven't even hit the spot...
Fabulous!
I think not.

Elucidation

I'm not sure who coined the term "ghetto fabulous" but I heard it everywhere I went. I was almost tricked into thinking the ghetto really was fabulous. Could I have been the only one missing the glamour? This made me take a look at my surroundings. My ghetto. The place I had been working so hard to get away from. Once I did take a conscious look, I didn't see fabulousness or greatness. I saw pain, struggle, and lack of social network, lawlessness, injustice, and broken families. Has it gotten so bad that we've become complacent? Have we learned how to be happy in these volatile environments? If so, then I object! There is a better lifestyle. In its current state, my ghetto does not represent fabulousness. And now that I have taken the time to see that there is a need for immediate change, I plan on doing my part in making that happen.

Vote

Change.
America is ready for change.
Key words
Endearing gestures
Woo America's people
Woo me
Vote!
Let your voice be heard
is what politicians force into the minds
of the unseen
The unrecognized
The faceless faces
Take your place in this
Free land
Free
What a contradictory word.
Show me this freedom that you speak of
Mr. Politician.
Show me this equality.
Don't sell me anymore dreams to
Win my John Hancock on your ballot.
I am human
I am human
I am human
Just like you

Elucidation

The politicians of today are fighting for our votes like I have never seen in my lifetime. Dramatic growth is taking place in America. We have a black man (Barack Obama) running against a white woman (Hillary Clinton) for the presidential nomination and both are leading the race. The Americas have come a long way I would say. There is so much excitement over this one fact alone that it is hard to actually understand what each candidate represents. Are they fighting for our benefit? Is this another form of trickery not unlike what was given to this nation by President Bush? Do they really see us this time around? Oftentimes we choose not to vote because of lack of understanding. Other times we vote without understanding what it is we are lending our voices to. The only reason we are not seen and heard is because we choose not to be. If we educate ourselves on the intricacies of politics, we can make a difference. Sitting back and blaming the politicians is no longer an option.

Music

Have you ever had something you were good at? Something you loved so much that you couldn't give it up if you wanted to. I had that something. It was music. Not playing music or singing it, but writing it. I wrote my first song at age seven. I called it "I Love You." Some of the lyrics went as follows:

Oooh
And you think that it's true
I love you
But I let someone else take over you
And it's true, it's true
If you know that it's true
Come tell me and you together
Together
Together we stay apart and live our lives.

Now as you can see, I wasn't making much sense at age seven. However, whether it made sense or not, my heart and soul still went into every word. So much so, I could still remember each of them today. I've made many attempts at trying to get myself heard, but unfortunately I didn't have enough support in my early years to really understand the value of my gift. I just kept singing and writing; showing family and friends. As an adult I continued this pattern concerning my craft. I would get an idea, write about it, and then share it with the people closest to me. I learned that my problems came with working to do this on a larger scale. I have pursued writing professionally a few times, but none of which I put 100% of my effort into following through on. Some ask, "How can you not aggressively pursue something that you love so much?" And I'd answer, "Fear." Not fear of failure, but fear of success. Sometimes it felt as if I would rather stay stuck in my rut because it was comfortable and safe. I didn't want to be challenged because it forced me to work harder than the norm. I became unmotivated and lazy because what used to be a challenge was now second nature and I wanted to stay in that comfort zone, the place where it seemed like life was easy. But this is how I became dormant. It was vital to the fulfillment of my life to pursue my passions wholeheartedly. When I didn't use what God had given me, I floated through life without a purpose, and in the end what I had to show for my life was either non-existent or meaningless. The choices I made shaped my life. I couldn't just accept what was being handed to me anymore. I learned to trust that what I had to offer this world was worthwhile, and once I did, doors opened for me and the rewards of doing something I was passionate about were far greater than any material possession.

MILESTONE

Intellectuals ask questions in search of the right answers.

Dummies remain silent,
hoping to appear as if they already know.
Idiots simply don't give a damn!

Risks

Is it worth it?
I'm not sure if it's worth it.
I think it's worth it.
I'm hoping that it's worth it.
Will the reward be worth it?
But what if it isn't worth it?
Is the worry of it all worth it?
Is the consequence worth it?
Is the experience worth it?
Is the loss worth it?
Is the gain worth it?
I don't know that it's worth it?
Is the fear worth it?
Is the courage worth it?
I want to know whether or not it's worth it.
But I'm not sure if I'm ready to know
          whether or not it's worth it.
Is the anxiety of trying to figure this out right now worth it?
Yes...

Elucidation

Sometimes what we want is right in front of us, but we spend so much time negotiating with ourselves that we let opportunities pass us by. There are times when we should just follow our hearts and take risks. The only thing on the other side is a success story or a lesson learned.

Money Woes

Twenty-five thousand dollars a year
My employer gives me with a smile
Proud to say he offers
Competitive pay
in return for me completing his day's work.
Days worked like I own this company.
I know all the ins and outs
The ups and downs
And was responsible for a half million
in gross profits last year.
My employer asks
Wasn't that this past year?
But even though I feel a raise is near
I haven't seen one yet.
Not wanting to feel like this is my end
I try to treat myself when I can.
A pair of shoes or new earrings.
Since I am trying to catch me a man.
But I digress.
I work
I work
I work so hard!
I deserve it.
I also deserve a corner office with a view
of the snow capped mountains.
But I haven't found
the courage to go get it.
Still behaving like someone is going to give it.
I AM going to triple my salary
But first...
I quit.

Elucidation

I am not the first or the last to feel stuck in a dead-end job. Working because we have to feed the kids, pay the rent or keep the lights on. But what we all want is to be able to do more with our finances than meet the bare necessities of living. The only way to do that is to put ourselves in a position to do more. Sounds easy, right? Well, it's definitely easier said than done. Experience has taught me that sometimes we have to sacrifice the things we have in order to get the things we want. The extra time used to watch television after work can be used to further education. Money being spent on trips to the hair or nail salon can be saved to join an investment group or start a business. The main idea is to be proactive about the things we want out of life. Every moment spent doing nothing is another moment trapped in mediocrity.

Entrepreneurship

Strength
wants to be born.
Torn from the womb
prematurely.
Surely
there must be reason
why strength couldn't
mature in its due season.
Seeming pleased in
the monotony of weakness,
she reeks of disappointing eyes.
Slaving to the white man's pen
is this woman's prize
as well as her demise.

Elucidation

My girlfriend, Sheila has worked since she was in the tenth grade. She went on to earn her Bachelor and Masters degrees. She makes a decent living and bought her first piece of real estate in her early twenties. On the outside looking in she lives a comfortable lifestyle. I am so proud of her and her accomplishments. I've asked her a few times what she wanted to do with herself now. I wanted to know what she loved. Her response was always geared toward starting her own non-profit. She loved helping people learn. She has all of the essentials to become a successful entrepreneur. Well one day, my girlfriends and I decided to go into a business venture together. We had this grand idea to start a speed-dating network in our area. We were all excited and promptly started putting our ducks in a row. We purchased our DBA, business licenses, and all the materials we needed to have a successful first event. When our opening night finally arrived we were prepared to entertain a maximum of 100 guests. Unfortunately, only seven people showed up. In my mind we were okay for the first night. I was looking forward to how our business would progress. What I didn't realize was that Sheila was having a nervous breakdown in the bathroom. My other two girlfriends and I went in to make sure everything was okay and she made it clear that things were not. In fact, she wanted out of the whole situation. She no longer wanted to be a part of Mate-A-Minute Speed Dating Services. I was very surprised by her response. She went on to say she made great money and did not need anything extra, so there was no reason for her to continue. Although we were all disappointed, we supported her decision. What I learned about my dear friend through this experience was that she had a desire to do more. She craved

the power of the pen, but she was afraid of failure. She imme-
diately reverted back to what she was secure in: her job and her
education. For her, one plus one equals two and there was no
logical explanation for why we didn't meet or surpass our
expected profit margin. What she was certain of was if she
showed up for work and fulfilled her expected duties, she
would receive a pay check at the end of her forty-hour work
week, and if she furthered her education, the odds of her
increasing her salary was greater. She was right. Her logic was
dead on and is the primary formula for becoming what society
deems a success. However, my friend has the potential to do
far more than make billions for corporate companies while
they pay her pennies. She is equipped with every tool to do that
for herself. Will she? Who knows? Maybe my opinions of her
capabilities are far from what she truly desires. My only wish is
that she is truly happy in her day to day. And if she is not, I
pray for her courage to fulfill all of her dreams.

I love you Sheila!

MILESTONE

From this day forward I will make my money work,
I will not let my money work me.

Woman

Being a woman is awesome
Getting lost in life's little gifts
Somehow lifts the spirit of us all
Woman
Summed up in one word
Derived of many intricacies
Some named
Others unexplained.
Woman
Nothing else compares to how it feels
To be a being of this nature
Nature itself leaves people to wonder
No wonder she is named Mother.
Oh the feeling is grand
To stand and be appreciated for
Carrying each generation up until this very moment
woman
life
I am
We are
Born to give it
And raised to live it!
Sometimes I just have to laugh
In this life
we were truly given the greater half!

Elucidation

This piece was derived from one of those days when I was feeling good about being feminine, being a woman. I was happy about being needed. I know women who feel like being just that is a burden. We do hold many titles and when we are not around our presence is evidently missed. My husband often says he is nature and I am nurture. When our children need special attention he looks to me to cater to their needs. When they just need a presence or someone to head the household he storms in and brings authority. I can be considered the calm to the storm in our household. Being able to have someone else take up some of the slack makes being a woman so much easier. However, when we have to carry the weight of it all, we seem to be able to do that flawlessly as well. What it is about the nature of a woman that allows us to be able to kick it into fifth gear whenever we are needed is a mystery. But I am so pleased to be a part of the chosen species to have that kind of exuberance.

Nicole

For Diane
A mother watching her child taken by cancer

Your eyes
are calling me.
So with everything in me I give.
Cause I too
want you to live.
My time
My hands
My breath if I can,
Cause I too
want you to stand.
I don't blame God,
although him taking you so early seems rather odd.
I blame the physicians
hiding behind this inequitable system.
Somehow the mere ability
to empathize missed them.
I wept
You wept
We wept
Till finally you slept.
My child
My best
Flesh of my flesh
My sorrow and rage
Will not let me rest
I'm fighting for you
Till I have nothing left.

Till I have nothing left.
Till I have nothing left.

Elucidation

This is yet another example of the silent killer: cervical cancer. I sat and listened to a mother tell the story of how she learned of her daughter's illness. She shared all the intimate details of how the doctors treated her child inhumanely because she could not cover certain expenses needed to keep her alive. After taking every avenue available to a mother fighting for the life of her offspring, Diane was at her wit's end. The time had come for the doctors to give what they chose to be their final recommendation: go home. Go home. Now considered terminally ill, Nicole was removed from the care of the physicians and taken home where she said her goodbyes.

It is so important to make health a priority in our lives. Some of us have insurance and don't use it. There are also those who are eager to take better care of themselves, but cannot afford health insurance. Women, we are dying. We are dying every day over things that can be prevented. Things that puts us at greater risk than cervical cancer. We must listen to what are bodies are telling us. For those of you who feel like you are completely out of options, let us know your story. We will do everything we can to help. We will make this world a better place...one person at a time.

I chose to keep this section précis out of respect for Diane and her family.

Me Against The World

The world is against me
So it's me against the world see
I'm a hater of things that are worldly
So I pause in my steps
And let the Lord lead
I use to believe that it was easy
To do only the things that would please Thee
But that was a lie in itself
And I just didn't know it
Cause to that chaotic world
My actions showed it
Yes, I used to talk that talk
And never walk that walk
I used to hear the Lord call
And be heated when my kingdom fall
Not knowing at the time
That my kingdom had not yet come
To make a long story short
I was smart but I was dumb
I was smart for wanting to know
But I was dumb cause I did not go
When God called me to the altar
To renew my faith
My spirit said go
But my flesh said wait
You're not ready for this
Just think of what you'd miss
Your plans for tonight
Or that C-note from Chris
So I prayed to myself

Lord I need some help
I want to follow you
And do my own thing too
Am I wrong?
Is the question I ask when I'm singing His praise
Cause I think of what I do on my ungodly days
I'm in a mess
But far less than what I used to be
I'm slowly coming out because I choose to see
That the world is against me
So it's me against the world see
I'm a hater of things that are worldly
So I pause in my steps
And let the Lord lead
Lord lead me in the right direction
I see the world coming so I need protection
My spirit is growing strong
But my flesh is still weak
So I don't need extra demons
That's why I'm careful when I speak
Cause they're lingering around
And they succeed with persistence
Just waiting on me to speak
Sinful things into existence
The God of this world is trying to work me
But he can't hurt me
If I work on being worthy
So I read my bible
And I fast and I pray
And I pray and I fast
And try to walk in his way
But listen ya'll it was harder than I thought

Cause when I had it together
That's when I got caught
Caught up in the world
Cause the world caught me
Slipping into worldly luxuries
I kept slipping on back
Most people call it back slide
Perfected masking my spiritual emptiness
With imitation pride
Again and again I kept multiplying sin
Not noticing the hole that I put myself in
Now, the deeper the hole
The more I felt my soul
Drift into the darkness
Cause I foolishly lost control
But now I want to come out
Heavenly father take my hand
Help me out of this
Cause now I truly understand
That the world is against me
So it's me against the world see
I'm a hater of things that are worldly
So I pause in my steps
And let the Lord lead
Lord turn me around
Cause I need a new start
Purge and renew
Create in me a clean heart
Pull me in your arms
And hold me real, real tight
Cause I've tried the arms of man
And they can't seem to get it right

Cause every time they let me go
I gain a feeling of regret
Then I come running back to you
Because you haven't failed me yet
That's why I love you more than me
My Jehovah –nissi
Jehovah-jireh my provider
That's why I stride like a rider
On the devil
Like the Panthers did in the 60s
And I'm gone keep on riding
Till the day you come and get me

Amen

Elucidation

Have you ever been in a place where you suddenly became aware of your spiritual self? I was. All of the excuses I developed for living or not living in God's will were now hidden in plain view. I realized that for a long time, what I was actually doing was being a hypocrite, liar, and any other variation of fake a person can think of. But God wanted me exposed. In spite of me, I was given understanding. I found out that what was desired of me was honesty. A truth that I had never lived in before. I was so busy trying to look the part for other people that I lost myself in the process. Playing up my successes and hiding my struggles was second nature. I became so astute that I thought that along with everyone else, I could fool my creator. But He had a plan that even I could not derail. For the first time in my life I was being forced to tell the whole truth regardless of the backlash. I discovered that in order for me to do that, I had to learn how to be honest with myself. I stopped living on religious expectations and asked God to show me what he wanted me to do. See, my experiences were supposed to help someone. I was ushered into trading in a polished character for a tattered one and it felt so good. It felt good to finally be all of me and not just a fragment. It was in this valued journey that "Me against the world" was birthed.

How Long?

How long will I continue to yield to temptation?
I've had heaping mounts of education
But maybe not enough demonstration
On how not to
I've got to
Spill what I truly feel
Cause God is truly real
And although it seems amusing
To just keep slipping and sliding
I've got to get off this ride
Cause it's tiring
To keep hiring and firing
And hiring and firing
The devil and his advocates
I have to get used to standing
Whether it be a man thing
Or a hand thing
If you know what I mean
I kinda want to let the Lord
Help me to deal with myself first
Instead of making a rebuttal out of
Some line that I hide behind
And might find
Pleasing to someone else's ears
Or easing to some one else's fears
Cause no matter how much I talk
My walk is still going to be my walk
And no matter how much
You recite to me Bible verses
And inform me of demonic curses

If I don't get in the spirit
And read it myself
I'll never hear it
And it'll be of no help
So with all due respect
You can't tell me about my flesh
Cause where I'm weak
You may be strong
And where my flesh is right
Your flesh may be wrong
So like I said before
I don't know how long
I'll continue to yield to temptation
I've had heaping mounts of education
But maybe not enough demonstration
On how not to
But I've got to keep trying
This is my faith
The bible says
Seek ye the kingdom of God
Not…
Find the kingdom
And once you do we could never be at odds
Cause nobody's perfect
And it's not worth it to make believe you are
Cause you're far from it I tell you
You're far from it I told you
And I'll sum it up one more time
I don't mean to keep repeating this line
But you're far from it
Take heed of the Pharisees
Who whore good deeds like a badge

And would give everything they had
To please God in another man's face
Blindly blinded from His mercy and grace
It's time to give up on this race of religion
And start relying on God
Cause religion has got us divided in groups
Downplaying the hoops and hollers of the Baptists
And the soothing praises of the Catholics
At this point in time
We need to intertwine
With one focus
Quote this...
Jesus is the head of the woman who wrote this
How long will we continue to yield?
If God is a healer
let Him heal
the desire to proceed with caution
and pause when our curiosities are fulfilled
if it's God will....
Give us all the power and strength to simply
walk away

Elucidation

Learning how to walk away from temptation is a daily struggle. I know people who offer every piece of sound advice they have, but can't seem to execute the very discipline they're so eager to preach. However, I am not offended by them because I understand them. I have lived on both sides of the fence. I had counsel for everything I felt was not righteous in others and my tongue was quick, but I hadn't much to show for all this wisdom. I had a hard time living it, but expected everyone else to. I am now practicing being the person to listen and not judge, but show someone else how God is working in my own life without pushing my choices and beliefs on them. The bottom line is that Gods' way is Gods way. All we need to do is carry out our part in making sure we are true to Him and then ourselves for our light to shine, and without words, others will follow suit.

MILESTONE

Every day I make it a point to be better
than I was yesterday.

Tall

You are light
in a room full of darkness
You spark this
energy that I have not yet seen duplicated
You created laughter in the souls
that were content in depression
You are a life lesson
My cousin
I'm lovin' everything about your spirit
I wish you were still here to hear it
Sunshine…
You were mine at times.
You had a swagger that was unmatched
It's no wonder you had the women clingy and attached.
Black
Confident
Tall
You had it all at your fingertips
Even when you were trying to come to grips
with the" hustle" and the "straight and narrow"
You managed to keep your eyes on the sparrow
You sang because you were happy.
People envied that about you
Always playing and joking
It's no wonder people doubted you
I mean….who could really take you seriously?
Especially when serious was not your style
I wish you could have stayed just a little while longer
But I'm stronger because of your passing.
It reminded me again that this life is not everlasting

So in your memory I will live more today
Give more today
And receive all that this life has to spare
But save me some room on heaven's dance floor cousin
Cause soon I'll meet you there!

I love you Cotrell!

In memory of my cousin Cotrell "Tall" Sanders

Spring

The seasons of our atmosphere
Weigh us down when they change
Rearranging our thought process to the left
Instead of right
But we always slide back
Back to the ways we were
In the days when we first birthed this union
Spring
Grooving in dark rooms
To reggae beats
And inhaling hymns of Leimert Park streets
No insecurities or impurities
Cause we weren't seeking situations
That would cause us to tumble and rumble
Although we did stumble
As all couples do
My focus was on the goodness in you
Harmonically reciprocating
You gave me more I gave you more
You praised me more I praised you more
Until we could never get enough
Unsatisfaction can be so tough
Like hot summer days
With limited shade
Plenty of ice water
But why bother
Because you'd rather have a damn glass of lemonade
Aggravated by the heat of our discussions
Keeping issues to ourselves to avoid repercussions
Shading our heat with lovemaking

Until it became too hot for that
Trying to find ways
To bring the cooler days back
Praying to God for vision
But his decision was to let nature take its place
Now faced with our own decision
Intuition whispers…
Take off layers
It'll cool you down
But in the end we found ourselves naked
Nothing more to hide
No matter how hard we tried
Truth had to come out
This is the season of doubt
Uncertainties of you and me
The direction of the breeze
Or the color of autumn leaves
Should I stay or should I go
Should I break him off like I did before?
I don't want interference in my personal life
But should I ask my family for advice?
The Lord said in the past to just be still
In time our true hearts will reveal
So we held our peace to let it role
Until our warm hearts turned to cold
Like a stormy night on Christmas Eve
With no presents to give
So why receive
Depriving ourselves from the gift of each other
Steadily ripping seams of what used to be lovers
And every ripped seam caused eyes to rain
And raised the pain of separation

Alongside desperation to love again
Soul to soul
And friend to friend
Back to back like soldiers
Is what I was told
And can now hold true when we slide back
Back to the ways we were
In the days when we first birthed this union
Spring
Grooving in dark rooms to reggae beats
And inhaling hymns of Leimert Park streets
No insecurities or impurities
Cause we won't be seeking situations
That will cause us to tumble and rumble
Although we may stumble
As all couples do
Your focus will be the goodness in me
And mine's…the goodness in you.

Elucidation

Spring represented the desire to make an old relationship feel like new after it had gone full circle. This was my first time experiencing the ups and downs of a serious relationship. I was in love, but I went from loving a man so much to where I just became totally consumed with him. So much so that I demanded every spare moment he had. I needed to be in his space. Every time he gave me what I asked, I later wanted him to go above and beyond what he had done before. I couldn't be satisfied. We soon grew irritated with one another. He'd leave for the day and I'd be relieved because being in the same room was draining. There were times where I'd be home and he'd literally be ready to push me out the door, pressing me to call my friends to do something. We argued often about nothing and nothing was ever resolved. Our behaviors triggered a whirlpool of insecurities. I had so much time to ponder while we were apart; I began to wonder what exactly it was he was doing. I started reading his journals, going through his clothes, and checking emails and cell phones for messages from other women. After all, if he wasn't spending time with me he had to be with someone else right? Right. Needless to say, I found everything I was looking for and he didn't deny any of it. It was almost as if he was happy that I now had a reason to want to let go; and I did. The withdrawal symptoms came suddenly. I couldn't eat, sleep, or think anymore. I didn't know what to do with myself, but I knew that I didn't want to suffer in the pain of heartbreak any longer than I already had. So I forgave him and went back within one week's time. We appeared to be a happy couple for a while before this cycle repeated itself multiple times. Each time a little more abysmal than the last. I was twenty-one years old and still wet behind the ears. What I didn't realize until much later was that my self-indulgent behavior had a lot to do with the disintegration of our relationship. Men are not attracted to dependency. In the process of learning how to love and coexist with him I lost myself. I wanted to do what he did, and be where he was for the sake of being together. But my needs and dreams were left by the wayside in the process. His life became my life and that is a formula for disaster. With practice, I learned how to love me first. How to not put my partner's desires before or behind my own. I now know how to be present in a relationship and have my very own presence at the same time.

What's Next?

Complicated?
Not really!
But my reality is that it really is…
It really is complex.
I never wanted to give you sex
I wanted to give you my eyes
Baptize you with my cries when I'm overjoyed
let you analyze my thoughts when I'm annoyed
Make you talk about the issues you try to avoid
I didn't want to give you sex.
I wanted to give you my poems and songs
Give you time to make right out of things that went wrong
I wanted to give you kisses and best wishes
I wanted to serve you hot meals on my lemon fresh dishes
I didn't want to give you sex.
I wanted to give you my smiles and laughs
I wanted to be your other half
Give you a silent night on a quiet beach
Give you any thing that was in my reach
I didn't want to give you sex.

Complicated?
Not really!
But my reality is that it really is…
It really is complex.
I never wanted you to be my ex
I never meant for you to be an ex factor
But somehow we twisted and turned
and somewhere down the line somebody got burned
somebody got scared to give what it was worth

somehow, someway...somebody got hurt
But I never wanted you to be my ex!
I wanted to erase this false illusion
And let you know if we had to reach some conclusion
I'd have you right here near my breast
Putting all of your issues and worries to rest
I never wanted you to be my ex
I wanted us to watch each other grow
I wanted us to vibe off each other's flow
I wanted us to go where we didn't expect to go
But above all else, I wanted you to know
I never wanted to give you sex.
I never wanted you to be my ex.
My question now is...What's next?

SHANET DENNIS 73

Elucidation

Picture this. You are sitting in front of the finest man you've seen in a long time. He cooks you dinner at his place and every corner is immaculate. (So much for the myth of the single man and his rundown bachelor pad.) After dinner, he kisses you softly; like he means it. While he simultaneously caresses and holds you tightly. This man doesn't want to let you go and you don't want him to. Then just when you think it couldn't get any better, he goes in for the kill. Wanting to preserve your lady-like image, you pull away slowly. He pulls you closer and this tug of war goes on for most of the evening. When it's all said and done; you have successfully made it through the first date without giving up the booty. You run home to tell your friends what a great evening you had and how well you two were vibing. Hours, days, and finally weeks go by with no call. Feeling a little concerned, you call your dream guy up only to hear that he's busy and has to call you back later. But later also turns into hours, days, and finally weeks. Not wanting to look desperate, you decide to send an email just to let him know you're still around. When he doesn't respond to your email either, you ultimately decide to let it go.

Months go by and you're still living the single life. Your phone rings and it's an unfamiliar number. Reluctantly, you answer and it's your dream man who dissed you for no apparent reason. After the usual small talk, you've built up enough nerve to ask what the hell happened. He explains that he thought the night was going well. He was so attracted to you and he thought you felt the same way. When you kept giving him the cold shoulder, he took that as a sign that you weren't really interested. Not wanting to play games, he moves on. You accept his response and move forward with the conversation. After hours of laughing and joking, you say your goodbyes and hang up the phone.

This is what happened to me. I didn't understand what was going on. I thought I had played my hand to the T. But things just did not pan out that way. I had time to contemplate our situation and in the process I gave birth to this poem. In it, I explained the plan I had for me and him. I tried to tell him what my desires were, and now that we had cleared everything up, I wanted to know what was next. When I recited this poem to my friend he gave me kudos, but he never responded.

In retrospect, I think this piece represents every woman's desire for a man that she's dating or would like to date seriously. Most times, we don't want to just give a man sex. We want the opportunity to give everything else we have; the things that make sleeping with him an added bonus.

MILESTONE

I am not the first woman to mother a child.

I will not be the last.

I am the best mother that I, only I, can be.

The Death of My Children

It was April of 1998. I walked into a room full of people. There were couples sitting hand in hand. Women young and old were waiting. The décor in the room was pleasing to the eye. There were no cold linoleum floors or uncomfortable seating. The walls were lined with sofas that had beautiful earth toned colors. There were lamps of different contemporary styles on solid oak end tables next to every sofa. I went to the reception-ist window and gave them my name. The young lady handed me some forms to fill, took my insurance and identification cards with a big smile, and asked me to have a seat. I sat, looked around, and began to fill out all the forms. I noticed that every person in the room had the same melancholy look in their eyes. It wasn't long before my name was called. The nurse gives me the same endearing smile as the receptionist did when she asked me to follow her. She asked me a series of questions. Do I smoke? Do I have any serious health problems? Have I had any other surgeries? Most of the questions I had already answered on the forms. She then handed me a sheet of paper and says, "Read this and if you agree, copy it as you see it and sign below." The paper read "This abortion is my choice." I did as she instructed. She then walked me into another room to change my clothes. Her work was done.

I was then greeted by another nurse with the same pleasant smile. I thought to myself, this must be in the employee handbook. She asked me to remove all jewelry, pull my hair back with a rubber band, and make sure I get completely naked. However, I could leave my socks on if I'd like. They provided me with a standard hospital robe and paper slippers. After disrobing, she took my vitals and sat me down across from every other woman waiting for their names to be called. I waited for about fifteen dreadful minutes before my chart was pulled. The third nurse that I was introduced to that day took me into another room to get my blood drawn. I was getting impatient. I couldn't stand the thought of not knowing what was next. The process was taking so long it was becoming scary. Again, I was asked to wait. The Ricky Lake Show was on television so that somewhat kept my mind off things. "Shanet Bennett" the forth nurse called. I headed into yet another room. I was asked to lie back on the table and place my feet in the stirrups. "Scoot down honey," she suggested, so that my buttocks would hang off of the table. As I lay there in all of my nakedness she remembers to cover the lower half of my body with a small white cloth. As she was giving me an IV, the anesthesiologist walked in from a door on my left that I didn't notice when I entered the room. "Good afternoon!" he says with more enthusiasm than I was ready for. "Are you ready to go night-night?" Before I could answer he told me to have a nice sleep and to count backwards from ten.

I woke up in pain. My cramps felt like the normal cramping I would get during periods. I notice I was not in the surgery room anymore. I was now in recovery. There were about eight other women lying in a row of beds. The woman to the left of me was yelling for her baby who was sucked out of her moments ago. The young girl on my right was just sitting and crying, with a dazed look on her face. She couldn't have been more than fifteen years old. Most of the others were still asleep. I was given a Tylenol for the pain as the nurse told me to lie back down. I was ready to leave. She felt I needed to rest awhile longer. About twenty minutes later I was given a maxi pad and was finally told that I could put on my clothes. I was glad it was over. I dressed and couldn't wait to eat. I hadn't had any food or water since midnight the night before. There was crackers and juice in the waiting area where we were all waiting on our rides to pick us up. Crackers and watered down Koolaid never tasted so good. The receptionist paged in to notify the nurse of my ride's arrival. I was given birth control pills and antibiotics on my way out the door. "Take one in the morning and one before bed with food until they're all gone. Have a good day. Get some rest," she said in a whisper.

In retrospect, it wasn't so bad. I came out unharmed. I had heard so many stories of women having serious complications like hysterectomies and even deaths during this procedure. Those images drove me crazy during the entire process. I prayed to God for forgiveness and vowed to never put myself through that again. Until of course, I got pregnant again. It was only four months after the last abortion. It felt like decades. My first was by Bobby who I spoke of earlier. My daughter was only a year old then. Outside of the morning sickness kicking my butt, I couldn't see myself toting around two babies. Some say my reasons were selfish. I agree. The second time wasn't any better. I tried to follow through with the pregnancy. Over a period of about two weeks I had lost about fifteen pounds. Hell I was only one-hundred eleven pounds to start. I couldn't eat anything at all. I couldn't even hold water down for more than two to three minutes at a time. Something had to give. I felt like I was dwindling away. I came to the conclusion that my body wasn't ready to carry another child. A week later, I was lying on a table letting yet another physician suck what would have been my third child out of me.

You would think I would have learned my lesson by now, right? Yeah, me too. It happened again. My third abortion didn't go as well as the first two. I went home immediately after the surgery as instructed. I didn't do anything abnormal. After lying down for maybe an hour I began to cramp so bad that I felt like I was in labor. I think I actually was. I called the emergency number that was given to me by the family planning facility and they told to me to come in immediately. After going through normal emergency room procedures, their conclusion was that I had a blood clot. Their remedy was yet another (abortion) D&C procedure. The doctor gave me antibiotics and scheduled an appointment for me the following day. My own conclusion was that they missed the baby the first time and therefore had to go in and do it all over again. What a price to pay huh? I was sickened by the whole situation. But after all, the abortion was "My Choice."

My fourth, fifth, sixth and seventh abortions went smoothly. Or maybe I had become immune to the torture my body was being subjected to. I'm not sure anymore. What I am sure of is that once I made that decision to follow through with such a thing it became so easy to do it again, and again, and again. At least, as many times as I deemed necessary depending on the circumstance. It can almost be compared to getting plastic surgery or a tattoo. It changed me emotionally and physically. I grew numb after each experience. I became prone to other self abusing situations, primarily with men. No, I should say…especially with men. I stayed in unfulfilling relationships. I took abuse in those relationships that no woman should. Now don't get me wrong, I am a beautiful woman if I do say so myself. But sometimes our self confidence is weakened by our experiences. Mine was. I didn't believe I deserved better. Allowing myself to be treated like damaged goods because that's how I felt. But no one knew how I really felt but me. I painted a pretty picture around my dead children. I laughed about it with friends. Joked about who had more than the other. Looking back, I am amazed at how casually we dealt with it. Although I am now proud and confident about who I am, I am a witness that no matter how good we make it look on the outside, the scars are still there.

Sunshine

He intrigued me
Indeed he wasn't what I was hoping for
But far more than I had ever imagined
Who would have thought that my mindset had then
The ability to drag him down
Sound
He spoke words of wisdom with ease
And seemed pleased to do so
I grew so much in that moment
When we were suspended in time
Rewriting the rhyme that I had so patiently written
The decision was made to recite it.
But before I could spit it
He made me bite it
And if I had to choose an emotion
I must say I was delighted
Still
I'm pleased with this feeling I feel
Grant it
I don't quite understand it
But I'm seeking understanding
In the process I'll try not to be demanding
And at best
Put my worldly propositions to rest
Because my dear sweet sunshine
I no longer want to be your TEST!

Elucidation

This was written about Sunny. I called him Sunshine. Not only was he handsome, but he had this way about him. He didn't say much outside of business and I respected him for that. To say I was physically attracted to this man would be an understatement. I was in a serious relationship at the time so I didn't act on any of the seductive thoughts going through my head, because I knew that if I had, he'd have been willing. Time passed and my boyfriend and I were no longer a couple. Sunny had left such a strong impression that the first thing I did as a single woman was dial his number. We talked awhile and he was fully aware of my intent. So I just came right out with it and told him that I wanted to sleep with him. Keep in mind that this was extremely outside of my character. He didn't hesitate to tell me that he was now a practicing Jehovah's Witness and saving himself for his wife. However, if I had given him this proposition three months before, he'd have been more than happy to oblige. With that being said, I saw a challenge. I went in full throttle and ready to break down this guard he had built. I had become a Jezebel. He agreed to me joining him and some friends at a local gaming facility. I walked in with my game face on. We laughed and had a few drinks. By the time the night was over I wasn't ready to go home and judging from his responses to my advances, he wasn't either. I followed him to his car because he felt as a gentleman he should drive me to mine. Before I could get in and shut the passenger door we kissed, and kissed longer, and kissed harder as the seconds passed until we were interrupted by parking lot security. I suggested we go to the beach and he was game. We arrived and parked in a secluded area. I was feeling a little bold and decided to mount him immediately. As our kisses turned into heavy grinding he stopped me, making it clear that he felt bad about what we were doing and didn't want to continue. Then he looked me dead in the eyes and said, "You are my Eve." The feeling that had come over me I cannot put into words. I was embarrassed and just felt small. I felt naked and wanted to hide myself just as Eve did when God had made her aware of her own nakedness. I had to take a serious look at myself to find out why I was behaving in this manner. Sunshine and I saw each other a few more times after that. I tried to compromise and get into what he was into because I hadn't developed a genuine interest. But we were indeed unevenly yoked. He was looking for a wife and I was looking for a rebound. My unresolved issues regarding my previous situation led me to be someone I didn't respect. Therefore, I could not respect him when he originally stated his position. I discovered that I didn't take the necessary time to heal because I was making decisions in my flesh rather than my spirit, and involving someone else not only created even more of a volatile situation, but it didn't speed up the process.

Love Loves Me

Once I had a love
Who nearly loved me to death
Had me holding my breath
To the things I wanted
Love taunted my desires
And threw large bodies of water
On the fires of my dreams
Sometimes it seemed as if there was hope
But…Nope
Same old ish
One time I tried to call it quits
But in a split second
Love was wrecking my flow
Touching me in places no other could go
Love had my brain
Filling me with sorrows
By promising tomorrows that never came
Love tricked me with his mystery
Because history… I mean his story
Was never the same
And somehow I was to blame
Adding to love's chain, chain, chain
Of fools that is
I didn't have love
Love had me by the throat
Nearly choked
But still able to breath
And that just isn't enough to make me leave
Cause love loves me
Love rubs me the right way

And love may sometimes darken a bright day
But that's all right
That's O.K.

My love keeps a time card
More often than not
Cause Sunday through Sunday
Love's punching the clock
Love's got
Two lives to live
A wife
Two kids
Two cribs
And after all that I get dibs
See I'm at the bottom of the pyramid
Giving strength to love
So love would have enough life
To live for his wife
And maybe enough to restore me
By the end of the night
Or early morning
Sometimes at the crack of dawn
Love would look me in the face
And remind me of my place
And disposition
In his circle of family and friends
And in my sadness love would
Try to make amends
By filling me with pipe dreams
And I do mean pipe dreams
Cause…
Is it really as good as I try to make it seem?

Maybe
But lately my focus has been strictly on the baby
And love.
Cause love loves me
Love rubs me the right way
And love may sometimes darken a bright day
But that's all right
That's O.K.

Love offered me a home
So I jumped right in
I jumped into love's life
And out of my skin
Love hinted for me to jump back in
But by that time
I was in too deep
Sleeping with the enemy
Love was the beginning of the end of me
I had to pretend to be a wife
That wasn't my role
That wasn't my life
Love took my life and cracked it in two
Then replaced it with some other woman's shoes
I couldn't fit them
Although I tried
In the process I may have lied
And cheated
But it was only so I wouldn't feel defeated
I wanted to strengthen my backbone
It was only a few dinners
And some chats on the phone
Ish...

I felt like I was doing me
But I was screwing me
Cause I knew love was in pursuit
To ruin me
But I still stayed
Lonely and underpaid
If only I knew love was a phony
He would've never gotten laid
See love spelled his name L-U-V
But love is incomplete without the O and the E
And since I didn't notice it before
Today it's that much easier for me to ignore
The fact that love loves me
Love loves me the wrong way
And love may sometimes darken a bright day
But that's all right
That's O.K.
Isn't it?

Elucidation

My girlfriends and I have had our share of staying is tumul-
tuous relationships. We often coached one another through
issues great and small. We have also had our fair share of
judging one another's decisions about staying in those relation-
ships. But always to no visible avail. Most times, just being able
to talk about it was enough. After listening to and telling the
same stories over and over, I asked myself if these situations
were normal. Is love supposed to feel caging? Is it supposed to
deplete a person's will to be themselves? Is it supposed to
demoralize? Are these types of relationships really acceptable
to us? Well, for a long time they were. I guess since we all had
our own levels of what we called a relationship, they became
tolerable. Maybe if we had an example of what a good man or
healthy relationship was, we would have had more fight to get
out of the fickle ones. Although it took some time, my
girlfriends and I did find a way out. One by one we watched
each other become stronger and more confident. And one by
one we learned how not to settle for what we had, but to go
out and get what we wanted and deserved.

MILESTONE

If it doesn't kill you,
It will keep trying...if you let it!

My Heart

This is my heart…
Nurtured and protected
Fed and neglected
Healed and infected
Then slowly reconnected to its original state
Love without the hate
Bend without the break
And free without the fake
"How much more of this oomph can you take?"
I mean free!
This is my heart…
Not phony from the start
But kind of fell apart toward the middle
Of my search for the truth
Blinded by the youth of this love
Thinking that it is what it is
And it was what it was
But it wasn't love yet
You and I hadn't even met
I knew your shell
And thought "well, well, well…
With this, I can be satisfied."
But after I cried and cried
I knew I had lied and lied
Thank God I'm talking past tense
Getting to know you became my last sense
And I continue in learning you daily
Baby, baby, baby…

Journal Entry

Having to make adult decisions can be difficult. For me it is. I am battling things in my life that I don't completely understand. Have I prayed about it? Not yet! Should I? Yes, immediately. I have been trying to talk to people about it but I haven't been completely honest with them. Which means if I get good advice; it may not be the best advice for my situation. This is my attempt at being as honest as possible. The relationship I'm in seems to be at a turning point. Be it good or bad, I don't know. I'm not genuinely happy in this relationship. The things that keep me holding on are superficial. He's handsome. He lives alone (even though his mom owns the place). He has a nice car. I couldn't imagine leaving him and someone else reaps the benefit of the growth he's had in our relationship. If our relationship doesn't work, whoever the next girl is is going to get a good man without the baggage. This is the stage I wish I would have met him in. Instead I went through the pain of his change which caused me to change. I think he is a great man, and with the exception of a few little kinks, we would have a chance at being happy together. But I just got a revelation. The way that I am feeling right now is not holy. It's not God-like and it's one of the Ten Commandments. Thou shall not covet thy neighbors anything. My whole reason for this relationship is that I desire the things he has and will have. I want to be a part of that.

July 7, 2003

It's funny how we feel from day to day. I don't know the date that I wrote the above entry. But today I feel totally different. I love this man whom I spoke of. We are still together and it's good. Granted, it could be better. But couldn't every relationship? I love this man genuinely if he has or if he has not. I want to build a family with this man. I have grown so much over the years that I understand what it is that I need and want in a relationship, and the reality is that I have most of that today. I am completely satisfied with where I am in my relationship. We are growing and coming to mutual understandings and it feels great. The process is great. I just thank God that it didn't take a life-threatening situation on my behalf to see that!

Elucidation

For the sake of having a man I became totally and utterly brainwashed. When God was not the head of me, my mind and entire life was full of confusion. If you don't agree, reread the previous journal entries.

Get Out!

I cried hourly,
wondering if I behaved cowardly
during this storm
considering...I was warned
once
twice
three times a charm.
It was only then that I felt the threat
of being harmed.
I became weak and distraught.
A ghost vision of everything my elders taught.
Behaving irrationally.
Confused by what he was asking of me.
Or demanding...
so strongly that I couldn't remain standing
as I should.
Who knew this man could
have this type of effect
on a woman who prides herself
on not standing in neglect.

Elucidation

He told me it was over and I needed to find somewhere to go. In my mind he couldn't be serious. I didn't want it to be over. I wasn't prepared for this breakup. Hell, I knew we had problems but nothing that we couldn't work through had we tried. A week passed and he asked if I had found a place. I hadn't. A month passed and he asked if I was saving my money. I wasn't. I guess one could say I simply avoided the situation as if it would just go away. It didn't. I watched him leave late at night and come home early mornings. Although he made it clear that we were no longer a couple, it cut like a knife to know he was dating other women right in front of me. We argued about it and then we made love. It only took a couple of days before he was out again and I was left home alone. It took a while, but I finally realized that this was the end and I was desperately in search of a way to reverse the inevitable. I did everything I was taught not to do. I cried, begged, bargained, cooked and cleaned, washed all the clothes, stayed home with his kids as well as my own, anything I could to make him want to change his mind. He didn't. I had become a skeletal existence of my true self out of pure desperation. I'm not totally sure what I was worried about. Being single, having to start over, losing him to someone else, or a combination of all of the above. But what I do know is fighting to hold on to someone who didn't want to hold on to me did nothing for my beautiful smile.

Missing You

Late nights
reminiscing on date life
Trying to be strong
so that I don't learn to hate life
without you.
Dreaming about you in the day so
daydreaming seems to have become my M.O.
My hopes and aspirations
of not wanting to let it all go.
Wanting to call you by the minute.
Wondering if your heart is still in it
or should I truly come to odds
with the idea of our love being finished.
Trying to come up with opening lines
only to realize
that I should have been the one leaving your behind.
Meditation
can make you remember things
like how you half-assed gave me my engagement ring,
unconsciously kept me from a life I loved
and told this caged bird
not to sing.
Oh Lord how I remember now.
How my tunnel vision
nearly kicked You out.
My focus was on him
that's why it didn't last.
That's why I needed to be kicked in my ass.
And I was kicked out.
So eloquently led by You.

If You hadn't pulled me out of him
who knows what I'd do.
I know now that I am free.
I no longer have to pretend.
I can now be all of me.
I no longer have to bend.
But I will always miss our good times
however far and in between.
I guess holding on to those memories
is what my missing you really means.

Elucidation

After being kicked out, I walked out of that relationship disappointed, hurt and confused like any other human being. I experienced the usual woes that take place when there is a major transition. Most would recognize this as the healing process. I missed my previous life so much that I almost made aggressive attempts at getting back there. But before I could do anything I had a revelation; a sweet epiphany I now call it. I realized that I had nothing to go back to. I had the opportunity to analyze my past relationship and learned that the bad times far outweighed the good. Because I was in a position where I had no one when I was used to having someone there, that aching feeling almost led me to accept and settle for anything rather than seek what I needed and truly desired. I found that remembering the old times isn't a sign to recreate them.

MILESTONE

I am a whole person with or without a man.

Simplicity

I don't need much.
Sometimes a gentle touch
is all I ask for.
All I need is
someone to make sure that my Trix never run low
because after all…
they're not just for kids.
I try to stay focused on the prize
in hopes that
God will send me someone who
sees me through his eyes.
I try to do the same
But I'm only human
Sometimes…
I can't help the urge to place blame
I'm working on that flaw
among others that can be changed.
I need an unconditional love,
Friend,
Ear,
Tear,
Shoulder,
Arm,
Heart,
Hand,
Smile,
Man.
Today I can say that I found this in you.
Today I can return this if you need me to.
Today God is blessing me.

Testing me
Touching me through you.
The baseline to this song written in spirit
God could not have chosen a better instrument.
No better way to make me hear it.
So perfect.
So infinite.
Even when I close my eyes
put down my pen
and close my mouth…
my heart can't stop singing.

Elucidation

If you ask for what you want, God will deliver. I was precise in my asking. I tried not to leave anything out. I wanted a man who was tailor-made for me. I wanted him to be handsome and humble, intelligent and considerate, and a multitude of other things. I wanted him to know me intimately. The way a man learns his woman. I wanted him to be spiritual in a way that he can't help but know that our union was ordained. I wanted that "I'm so happy we found each other" feeling. I needed that "I can't wait to get you home because you are looking good in that dress" type of love. All I had to do was ask. I can't believe I wasted so much time picking and choosing men that weren't right for me. But when I took the time to simply ask God to send me the perfect mate, he showed up with impeccable timing.

Honey

You take me to that quiet place
In a world full of thunder
And every time I fall into you
You just pull me under
You snatch me up
Wrap me up
And cover me
I've fallen in love.
And I can't hide it from the world they see it
If there are any other girls so be it
They can't have you now.
I'm like a bear and baby you're my honey
On a spring day when it's warm and sunny
 I want to dip my fingers in and taste
Pour you all over my face
And lick you real slow so you can stick.
Golden brown thick…Honey
You're the sweetest to me
And I'll let you drip off the sides of my lips
And fall all over me
As long as you keep on sticking to me
I'm gone keep on licking you like a bee
And there we'll be…
Stuck together like words to a melody of love
on a silent night that you created.
Cause you are my quiet place
In a world full of thunder
And every time I fall in to you
You just pull me under
You snatch me up

Wrap me up
And cover me
I've fallen in love

Elucidation

Not everything needs an explanation...

I Love You

Black Man I love you
I love you, I love you
I love you, I love you
Black Man I love you
I love you, I love you
I love you, I love you!

Your strength is something that I need
Don't leave
Some people are saying
that you are a dying breed.
They're saying it won't be long
That soon we'll look up
and the Black Man will be gone.
Please say it ain't so.
There's a lot of life ahead
and I need you here to help me grow.
Assist in sowing this seed I sow
Black Man don't leave me here
cause I wasn't meant to do this alone.
Some say you don't have a reason for breathing
but I gotta feed'em the TRUTH
Black Man I'm here.
And I'll do what I gotta do
to put strength where there could be fear
FEAR ME NOT!!
I'm not the one that's trying to break you down
or take you for your pot of gold
Black Man I'm your backbone
The other half of who you are

Black Man you are my shining star!
Your role is not in vain
Black Man I've been sent here to keep you sane
together it's easy to maintain
but first you must remember your name
BLACK MAN
you are my reflection
you're my protection
you're my comfort
you are…
just alright with me!
So be bold about your right to be
A BLACK MAN!!!

Elucidation

Black man I love you. This has to be said more often than not. Black men, our men, need to be uplifted in order to know that we still see them as more than what statistics state they are. Jail bound, unemployed, deadbeat fathers, down low brothers, and so many other negative connotations. They hear enough of it on a daily basis and although those men are out there, they are not the total makeup of the black man. It isn't rocket science. The last thing one should do is kick a person when they are down. My man loses his job and becomes a freeloader. If I decide to make the money and let him stay home with the kids, he's lazy. If he's working too many hours, he's neglecting the family and/or cheating. If he's in the wrong place at the wrong time, he should have known better. Can our men get a break? It seems to me that they can't win for losing. There are a multitude of black men that give a damn about a black woman, and understand that her contribution to their lives is far greater than any other could come close to. We should encourage that and let them know that we feel the same way. I'm not just referring to our lovers. I'm talking about the black man loading our groceries and offers help to the car. I'm talking about the man next door who fixes things when we are living the single life. I'm talking about the brother who sees us heading out to work everyday and never fails to tell us how gorgeous we are. Our men are awesome and they need to hear from us. Let's make it our business to tell them again and again how much we love and need them.

Internet Dating

I can't stay behind the screen
I've had too much
"Hey, how you doing?
Can I roll with you?
And, you can at least say hi girl
don't be so mean!"

I can't see behind words written
in Arial fonts.
I can't sense the need.
Can't feel the want
I want unforgettable smiles
And big *stick* walks to haunt me
I want to be haunted!

Please tell me you're single
cause I've been watching you mingle
from my VIP setting
Pondering thoughts of you wrapped
in my bedding
and that thing that you do
after every song...
I simply can't find in emoticons!

My flirts can't be seen
by the click of a button.
I've got a dimple in one cheek
And a switch in my butt,
And a cute little way that I say
"You know what?"

And you feel it when I'm feeling you
So there's really no frontin'

I can't stay behind the screen.
Kinetic energy cannot be keyed in.
I can't stay behind.....
I must put the screen
behind me!

Elucidation

When technology allowed me to sit at home in my pajamas and mingle with men I was all in. I had just come out of a long-term relationship and didn't have the energy to get dressed, let alone exert enough energy to look spry in front of potentials. Therefore, Internet dating became my new daily ritual. I would go to work, come home, eat, and get on the computer. Not to mention the times I used my lunch hours to chat. After talking for a short two weeks, I was always ready to meet. There was no way I could chat with someone for months on end with no face to face. I usually met them all at bookstores, restaurants and coffeehouses. Needless to say, they never turned out to be what I had expected. Not to say they were repulsive, just not quite my style. It didn't take long for me to figure out that the online dating thing just didn't work for me. It took away the opportunity to spawn instant chemistry. Online, it always seemed manufactured. I know this form of meeting people has spread like wildfire and people not only love it but have become addicted. As for me, I'm sticking to the old-fashioned way of meeting men. It's been working in my favor!

Foreplay

I can't hear him talk
I can only see his lips move
wanting to feel my hips groove
with every motion
moisturizing his lips like lotion
I'm
trying to keep my desire for him subliminal
my throbbing to a minimal
and although I can't hear him talk
I can't seem to contain myself when he walks
that big *stick* walk!
His body's calling me and I hear it
but I'm not afraid to admit that I fear it
I understand the thought of getting near it
can be fatal for me.
the idea of this big stick cradling me
can make me dependent
turning him into a plaintiff
and I the defendant
fighting for the right to have it all to myself.
So I cross my legs
and turn my ass to the left
cause he feels just a little too right.
now he's crooning me in the middle of the night
sending melodic shocks with every key stroke lightly
wrapping me around his little finger tightly
I might be sprung if he hit it from the back
while he bites me.
He excites me in ways
I can put in a simple phrase

but it's the kind that gives me aftershocks
after 3 or 4 days.
having me spilling what I'm feeling
for my man in all praise
Can I get an Amen?
Say baby…
When can I get some of that 'ish again?
some of that no sleeping
wine drinking
hey baby what are you thinking?
you kind of remind of my jeep and
baby just stop me if I go too deep
cause I don't want to do this if you ain't ready…
so I slowly reached down to unsnap my teddy
thinking…damn I should've confirmed whether or not we
were going steady!

Elucidation

This man was gorgeous to say the least. Tall, dark chocolate, bald, and had muscles that could make any woman do a double-take. His smile was infectious and he knew it. There was just something about him where one couldn't tell if he was giving off confidence or arrogance. At this point, I didn't care either way. After our first brief encounter, we successfully made it to our second date (maybe I should call it a meeting of the minds). He came over to my house smelling Zest-fully clean. He had intentions of showing me his talents so he brought over his keyboard and a pint of Hennessy. We talked for a while. I remember him mentioning the type of music he was interested in, but not much past that. I watched him intensely from head to toe. Although I had a difficult time hanging on his every word, I had no problem following his motions. He decided to play a song for me. I have no idea what he played but I know it was not only beautiful, but arousing. I laid there on my living room floor and let this man envelop me in a way that no one has before. Lost in blind lust, I was open. In retrospect, he knew what he was doing. I must give him kudos for doing it so seamlessly. He went from playing his own music to putting in one of the hottest CD's at the time and met me on the floor. He kissed me. He bit me. And between the two of our chocolate bodies, we made black history that night. However, when it was all said and done and the sun had risen again, he was gone and I was left with emptiness and regret.

MILESTONE

Sing a song every day on purpose.

Expectations

Patiently waiting
Pacing and saying to myself
I'm going to know tonight.
Keep it slow and light
Give my boo a bite to eat
and slide my feet right into his lap
Let him massage me into a temporary nap
Perhaps...
return the favor
as I do have Destiny's Child
teaching a sister how to cater to the right man.
Oh yes!
I do have high hopes for tonight's man.
He arrived and his scent was enticing
and the fact that
his hands were full was the icing between my lips
Trying to remember the tips my girls gave
on how to avoid the drips
So I walked away.
Asked him about his day
and inhaled every breath he used
to say what he had to say.
"Is Zinfandel ok?" I asked
Thinking...please don't pass
Wanting to use every excuse I could
to let him wax this ass!
This had to be more than a physical attraction
Cause we were talking and laughing
Kissing and grabbing
Boasting and bragging

And, hosting got put on the back burner
Shit, I was ready for some Ike Turner
Hoping He would grab by the back of my hair and recite
Bitch, you better sing that song right!
Aggression is what I was feigning that night.
I was leaning into him apprehensively like I was scared
And I was really daring him to push the limit.
If only he had he would have been all in it.
But we laid together
Made together what felt like waves together
We craved together
Bathed in what felt like raining intimacy
So the key to guiding him into me must be….
Hmm!
What might have been is a mystery to me!

Elucidations

Okay. Okay. I learned from my last encounter with the choco-
late Adonis. I decided to take the scenic route this time.
Wanting to enjoy the process of getting to know someone, I
made plans to wait before getting too hot and heavy with
anyone else. Still living in the residue of my online dating life, I
met Nigel. He was my Italian stallion. We met face to face at
the bookstore and headed for dinner from there. He was a
perfect gentleman the entire evening. Our relationship pro-
gressed at a snail's pace. We didn't kiss on the first date.
Although we talked often, I didn't let him know where I lived.
We met at public places whenever we went out on dates. I
eventually had dinner at his apartment and soon started
meeting him there. I admit I was proud of myself for my new-
found discipline, but almost two months had passed and I was
hot as a lit firecracker waiting to pop. I had made up my mind
that I was going to get me some just as soon as I could get him
to my house. I called him and told him that I was cooking
dinner and gave him the address. From the sound of his voice
his excitement was almost as high as mine. I made the neces-
sary preparations. Took my daughter to my mom's and had a
long hot bath while my food cooked itself. I was still bathing
when I heard a knock at the door. Dripping wet and smelling
like roses, I answered. He greeted me with a bouquet of roses
and two gift certificates to my favorite burger joint. My first
thought was that he was a great listener. I seated him in my
candlelit living room while I went to dry off. We had been so
G-Rated for the past few weeks that I wanted to heat things up
a bit. After drying I straddled him in my nakedness. The
spontaneity alone made for a great appetizer. It was less than a
minute of kissing and slow grinding before I crawled away

from him to fix his plate. I couldn't have written a better script! We ate dinner slowly. The whole time I was licking my lips and using every flirtatious gesture I could think of, but this man wouldn't budge. I couldn't decipher whether or not he was nervous or if he just didn't get it. Eventually we got into kissing and heavy petting. Ten minutes, twenty minutes, thirty minutes went by and still nothing. My lips were chapped and my feminine area was tender from grazing against his jeans. The fire dwindled and I had come to odds with the fact that what I thought was going to happen, simply was not. Our night ended with a hug and a gentle kiss.

Unfinished Business

I'm excited to see you.
Our last union was not enough
to satisfy my wanting.
I'm wanting more of your breath
My inhale to your exhale
until there is none left.

Elucidation

Expectations fulfilled.

A Tribute to My Man

You are life after death
A lingering breath of fresh air can't compare
You must be oxygen!
Packaged and locked into your being,
then sent to me by God himself.
You deserve more than what's left of me
You need the best of me
The rest of me will benefit from opportunities to
imitate your loving nature.
You are questions answered
A tired body pampered after a long day's work
Hope for the woman scorned
An example to the little girl warned of all the Mr. Intentionals,
conditions in relationship and a love unconditional.
A provider in ways far deeper than material possessions.
Your actions parallel your words
I no longer have to ask many questions…
I rest in knowing that you embrace me emotionally
and chase me the way a man courting a woman should.
My God it feels so good!
I didn't think chivalry existed anymore.
I was almost getting used to buying my own meals,
opening my own doors.
You are a man who makes a woman feel like a woman
Femininity is not lost when I am with you.
I feel rejuvenated!
Like God has blessed me with the chance to give birth to
"Something New"
So I can say this with every new breath…
You are life…after death!

Elucidation

After being lost in so many dead-end relationships I had finally found the one. The one I had asked God for in detail. You know how it feels to just live day to day in a monotonous situation? And then, to experience something you thought was impossible because it seemed so out of reach? If not, I will be the first to tell you until one has experienced the bad, there is no way to fully appreciate the great. I'm talking about something as simple as a touch on the hand while riding down the street. Someone who likes the same television shows that I do. Someone who understands my humor so I'm never laughing alone. I've got someone who doesn't mind cooking the meals sometimes. Someone who recognizes when my smile is upside down and immediately goes to work on doing something about it. These are things I didn't know I was missing because I was used to watching my shows in a different room. I was used to being touched in the bedroom and being close only when there are other men around. I laughed alone unless I was away from home. I cooked, but never enough to satisfy my mate's needs. And on those days when I just couldn't do it we ate out. I was satisfied with that. It wasn't all good, but it wasn't all bad either. Oh, but now? What I have now is great. What I have now makes me want to wake up early and stay up late just to lay there next to him in a conscious state. What I have now has given me a second wind. Wheeeeeeeeeeeeeeeew! I've been alive all this time, but now I am living.

Evidence of a Man's Mouthpiece

He loves me.
This I know!
For every day he tells me so.
Sells me so much hope for the future
and when solidity is questioned
he becomes a soother.
Smoother than silk or linen
he sweetly reminds me that we
are still in the beginning.
Then he…..
Kisses me on my chin and my waist
then races to get a taste of my sunshine.
In hopes that I remain fine
till he makes up his mind.
He likes to walk on beaches
Teaches history of the things I know not
I know not what lies behind his eyes
but I know when he lies behind my thighs
he's satisfied.
Glad that I gave him the opportunity to love me.
He puts no other above me
I AM HIS…..girlfriend?
The courtship is over
We can now be more than friends.
God has stepped in
We can now lay flesh to flesh
and skin to skin
I am his world.
For I have finally earned the GIRL!!
Our love is limitless

until he reaches his limit, it's
cool for now
for I am learning how to settle for less than I desire
because I am still on fire for this man.
My quest is to make him my last
but his last suggestion was to do things in its proper sequence.
See, since… love, marriage and consummation didn't suffice
he thought it would be nice to make it fit.
Consummation, Love, Marriage???
I think that was it!!!
He is like no other
Set apart from the brother that wants to hit and run!
He likes to hit and uummm…..
commit to hitting.
At least that's what I seem to be getting.
but I am not confused in this love
I don't feel used in this love
nor am I accusing this love of my uncertainty.
I certainly carry some weight in where we are to date.
I am confident in knowing that I have my three fourths/ ¾
That's the reward of a woman who knows her WORTH!!

Elucidation

A man has a way of making a woman feel like a million bucks when her net worth is two cents. He can make her feel like the pimple in the center of her forehead is one of her best features. I know it sounds funny but there are some slick talkers out there. I would ask some of my male relatives how they would get women to buy those cars, clothes and jewels and they always answered "I've got a mouthpiece." I used to laugh at them and blow it off as the usual riff until I noticed that I had been hypnotized by the mouthpiece myself. I had already asked God for my husband so I was in hunt mode for quite some time. I kept my eyes and ears open for his arrival. Every man that crossed my path was a potential and I was not going to let him slip through the cracks. So, to keep with the theme of a lot of my poetic pieces, I met a man. I presumed he was the infamous "One." He seemed to have everything I was looking for. He was educated, handsome, independent, and catered to my wants and needs. Now, if you haven't figured this out yet, I am an "in the moment" type of person. I love to take risks and do things out of the box. Therefore, I played by those rules regarding my dealings with this man. You might remember him. His name was Nigel. We had fun. Our time spent grew into love and admiration. Eventually, I grew sick of playing house and wanted him to step his game up. I needed something to show that he was in this for the long haul. We talked marriage heavily. He assured me that we would get there as soon as he got his degree. We talked children. He was certain that he wouldn't be ready for another three years minimum. In other words, he was comfortable with where we were in the relationship and wasn't ready to change that. He was all but blunt about it. He was so passionate and sweet with his words that it was hard to read the underlying message. I AM NOT GOING TO MARRY YOU ANYTIME SOON. I JUST WANT TO FINISH SCHOOL AND HAVE SEX WITH YOU ON MY DOWN TIME. Well, maybe he didn't mean in it in such a harsh way but that's what he showed me. Once I realized I was being bamboozled, I couldn't blame him. I made the decision to bring him home. I made the decision to sleep with him. I made the decision to not put God first when it came to my dealings with him. I made the decision to keep him around when I realized I was not in love with him. It would be too easy to say he tricked me into a dead-end relationship. The truth is that I let *stuff* control how I handle myself in that situation. I let my desire to want to be touched by a man lead me into a position where I was no longer seeking God. I put my wants in front of Him all the while blocking the gateway for Him to give me what I needed. I forgot what I was worth. Once our relationship ended, it didn't take long for him to make attempts at working his way back into my life. But fortunately enough, I had grown a little bit during our time apart and had to graciously decline.

MILESTONE

Forgiveness can heal a million wounds.

Reasons

I didn't walk away by choice
I could just hear it in your voice
Distance.
Resistance to what I was attempting to pursue…
YOU.
I extended myself to you and you pulled away
I pretended to be aloof
But my heart wanted to stay.
let uplifting words come out and play
and leave the heavy conversation for another day.
Remember WHY
and build on that…

But you pulled back!

I had…
a desire to see you
breathe you
at this point I needed you to embrace me
face me and lace me with reasons why we are stronger
than our current condition…
take a moment to listen to our hearts
and let that push us to a higher position.
Intermission is best left for those who have time to wait.
Breaks are for those that are tired
and are no longer fired up about what lies ahead

A love that weak…is better off dead!

I loved loving you

though for a month I felt caged
silencing myself to eliminate your rage
not wanting you to feel like you were constantly on stage
and overlooking the consequence my tongue would engage.
Feeling bottomless
like my pain has no end
this isn't easy going through heartbreak again
but it's a lesson learned
which for me is a constant
making it look effortless is my only profit

Is it over?

I can't say…
I can't truly be sure
the worry of it all I choose not to endure
I'll cry tonight
but look to smile in the morn
knowing there is nothing solid in a mind that is torn.
I love you today
Tomorrow I'll love you still
at this point our future
is left to God's will.

Elucidation

We've all experienced that pivotal moment when we have to involuntarily say goodbye to the one we love. It's a normal part of the circle of life. A test we'd rather not take, but must in order to grow. In this poem I was disappointed that my current boyfriend would just up and leave without a fight. We hadn't been seeing eye to eye for a while and he had finally reached his breaking point. He could see there was something wrong and would often ask me to talk to him about it. I couldn't. I didn't know how. I loved him, but I wasn't in love with him and it showed in everything I did. It had finally gotten to a point where I couldn't hide it anymore. I was angry for no reason. Everything he did was annoying. Sometimes just his simple presence would upset me. How do you tell a person something like that? Well, I didn't have to. He finally decided to remove himself from the situation. I admit I was shocked. I didn't think he would do it; cold turkey at that. When I realized he didn't want to have anything to do with me I called more. I fought harder. I wanted him to want me back. I couldn't understand what made him different from anyone else. He didn't budge. This poem was my last attempt at getting him to respond to me. I wanted him to give me something. I wanted him to show me a sign that I still existed in his world. It took a couple of weeks, but it worked.

Decision

He wants to lay with me
that's all that's on his mind
In me he lives
His undivided attention is what he gives.
Time
is of the essence
He's second guessing my sincerity
my pace is forcing him to need more clarity
Clarity has been given
he asked
and I have risen to the occasion.
The power of persuasion
is what he offers
but I will not accept
I intercept his gesture with truth
Uncompromised.
He doesn't believe that I feel the same.
Future.
Still, it seems his fire is tamed.

Elucidation

We talked, Nigel and me. Once I figured out the reasons he left and my reasons for wanting him to return, I gained clarity. I realized that he was not the one for me and I was still searching for what I needed. I explained to him that I wasn't ready to jump back into the type of relationship we had before. In all actuality, I didn't want to get into a relationship with him at all. I explained to him that I was seeing other people and wanted to see where those connections would take me. He seemed to be fine with that for a while. But his actions spoke differently. He called often. He wanted to see me more often. He made it clear to me that he wanted to win my affections over anyone else. I appreciated him for his pure desires. He was so sincere and that type of sincerity is hard to come by, at least for me. I couldn't see myself leading a man on who had such a clean heart. I knew, even before I had found what I was looking for that he would not be it, but I wanted to be gentle regarding his feelings. So I sat and wrote this for him, with him, and about him. It wasn't long before he got the picture, and he moved on with his heart intact.

Impatience

Patience is a virtue.
but if you don't hurry up
I'ma hurt you.
work up a sweat just trying
to get you to feel an ounce of regret.
I depended on you for something so minute
that it should not have been hard for you
to follow through.
but you had me waiting
pacing and saying to myself
this will never happen again
I will never ask him again for
a pot to piss in.
thought that this friend was die hard
but he didn't even try hard
I'm scarred from his negligence
but my elegance wont allow me act irrationally.
so I rationalize
I've come to the conclusion that
my importance to this man is only my illusion.
This friendship I thought had grown into a kinship
has digressed into an association
procreation of our past union is now stagnant
this would never have happened
if he hadn't said he was on his way in the beginning
and to think this all started because I asked him
to bring me a lemon.

Elucidation

Every time I come across this poem I laugh. It was written out of total frustration. I had asked my good friend Tarri to bring me a lemon and a bottle of zinfandel for my dinner. He told me he would be at my house in thirty minutes. I was pleased to know that I didn't have to leave my apartment and go out into that cold winter air. Thirty minutes, one hour, two hours went by and this man shows up with my wine and no lemon. I could have screamed I was so angry. The poem was a way for me to vent while I waited. I showed it to him when he arrived and we both were tickled to death.

Revelations

Longing for your presence.
The essence of Q.
In a matter of seconds
segments of you
have been engraved in my mental
There was power in your stance
and a swagger in your dance
that I could not keep confidential
I had to tell the world
So I started with my girls
explained how in a room full of ice
I somehow found a pearl
A rarity
That in one moment lost in your eyes
I could find clarity
whether it be
Temporary or without end
I will not tend to dwell
I would rather bask in the thought
that…. TONIGHT…. I know you well
a release to the jezebel
and a helpmate for this virtuous woman
that's planning on hurting you with somethin'
when the timing is right.
keeping sight of the grand scale of things
I'm well with things moving at a turtle's pace
cause as the story tells it
it was he who won the race
Stay with me Quincy
you have not crossed paths with a soul that is empty

and just to put it simply
You send me...
Swangin' like mint-condition
ish I got a list of positions
with your name on it
You could put a stamp and a frame on it
cause they were definitely inspired
by my imagination of yours truly!
Lord I hope this man is ready to do me...
right like
Joseph did Mary
and it's kind of scary when reading into it this deep
But peep...
I'm on a mission for submission to this man
but only if his decision
is to be submissive to a higher being
and after seeing that this is true
there is no limit to the things
he and I can do
And it feels likes oooooooooooooooh
But you don't know my name
I told you it was Bennett in the beginning
but in the ending I'm aiming to be Mrs. Fleming
Ha...
I might have to be number two with it
but that's because number one didn't know what to do with it.
Her mama should've took her to school with it
but I am ever so cool with it
As I am reaping the benefits
of her tactless behavior.
Fools rush
so I will savor every moment

hone it
until it's known that
this is a ride or die type situation.
Heavy meditation leads me to believe
that you are the truth
so in the youth of this union
I hope I don't ruin
the mystery
when I say
any other will soon be part of your history!

Elucidation

I told you before that I was on a hunt for my husband and I wasn't letting anyone slip through the cracks. It was the day before New Year's Eve and my girlfriends and I were partying at a local nightclub called Monte Cristo. We arrived at about 12:45 am and closing was at 2 am. We all knew we didn't have much time to waste if we were going to get our boogie on. I bought myself a drink and explained to my girls that I was about to dance with ten different men and everyone was going to get five to ten minutes depending on whether or not I was interested. My goal was to maximize my time. I finished my drink and was off to the dance floor. A half hour had passed and I had made it through four potentials. When I met number five he had magnetism. Especially considering that he wasn't my type at all. We danced, and danced, and danced some more. I spend the rest of my evening on the dance floor with this man. We exchanged names and interests over loud music. When the night ended we tried to hang out but I guess the stars weren't lining up for us that night. However, the following night we managed to make the time to spend together. We hung out, talked, and like any other man in the late hours of the night he tried to lay me down. I dodged that bullet with class and grace. I should have run for the hills at that time but I was intrigued. There was something behind his eyes and I wanted to know what it was. So I continued with the game of cat and mouse. We talked often and went out twice a week. I was into him because not only was he attractive, but he made me laugh. He was carefree just like me and that was fun. I mistook fun for common interest. I assumed we wanted to the same things because we responded to each other identically. My mind was made up. I was going to pursue this man and have him as my own. I was so confident about it that I wrote to him and told him what would happen. This poem was my revelation to him.

Untamed

I want to make love to your mind.
Grind until we've connected in ways
that no other has taken the time to graze.
I want to misbehave
Elude the tamed conversation that
we've been programmed to speak
I'm on fire to leak
confidential information as long as we
keep it between the sheets.
Or any place that is meant for the
"You" and "I" of this union
You done did what you do and
curbing my enthusiasm is not an option
I'm hot when
locking bodies is a secondary focus
I'm into locking minds
Quote this.
There is a method to my madness
What I'm giving you is truth
No other has had this
it's been inspired by you.
So while you roll with it...
I'm gone lose control with it
I'm all in
blind giving 110%
For only the grown and sexy knows
how to put this kind of stank on it!
Feels good don't it?
So unorthodox.
I love letting love outside of the box!

Elucidation

Quincy and I played with each other using our words. The next time I saw him he had written a poetic response to "Revelations" entitled "Roll with it." I was pleasantly surprised. I hadn't had anyone respond to me in such a rhetoric manner before. In his poem, he explained that he didn't know what to expect but he was going to roll with it and see what happens. Keep in mind, I was giving him my one two-punch. Because of what he had written to me I responded in the same way. I didn't want the conversation to end. It was fun!

Mind Games

Can I be honest without being hurt?
I'm not too sure if this could work
in such an adolescent stage
such an adolescent phase in this union.
Wanting to withhold pieces of me
but these pieces could be
key in what makes this true.

Who am I to you?

Our brains ask questions
that our tongues won't touch
in fear of feeling like we're asking too much.
basking in what feels like lust
but is just …..
a deep desire to know!
That fire to grow into something more than
"Yea I broke that nigga!"
"Yea I f--ked that hoe!"

Visions of white dresses and linen suits
walking barefoot on beaches
and tossing the boots
embracing the roots in which we
came to the point where we're saying
I DO!

I do love the idea of growing to love you

and doing the things that people in love do.
and putting none other than God above you
and enjoying the process of keeping it new!

Elucidation

These were some random thoughts. There is always a game played when it comes to dealing with the opposite sex. We try to deny it but it's true. There is a fear that a lot of us have of being completely vulnerable because we know how careless others can be with our hearts. To lay it all on the line takes courage. A lot of people I know feel that taking that risk isn't worth the heartbreak. But answer this question: is taking the risk worth the reward?

No Worries, Just Concerns!

He lingers in my mind
like a childhood memory
forcing me to remember things
that I didn't know had significance.
Gio scents
mark the pillows in my bed
as if this man thought far ahead
and had every intent on marking his turf.
Triggering thoughts of my worth
and wonder
if he knows what that is.
If he can see me.
Or am I simply making it too easy?
Is it okay to just be me
without him taking advantage
or taking for granted what I have
chosen to bless him with?
I'm guessing with everything he's
given me...
I'm driven to be scared.
Scared of what is and what isn't.
What did and what didn't.
And torn between what has
and has not been consistent!
Specifics aren't needed
if the above said words are heeded.
But speaking of necessity,
I've given him my weekday love
but what about the rest of me?
Although it all feels right...

If I had a preference
I'd reference the last few weeks
and ask him to give me his weekend nights.
However, I'm uncertain of my rights
in relation to him
because my situation with him is still young
I'm not interested in scaring him
just daring him to believe that I'm the one.
And behave accordingly!
And behave accordingly!
And behave accordingly!

Elucidation

I was still talking to Quincy. I was reading him. By this time we had established that we weren't seeing anyone else. However, we weren't in a relationship either. He was consistent in his behavior. He showed up two to three times a week, but always in the morning or early evenings. On nights when he did stay late, he was always gone by 2:00 a.m.; club hours. He was also consistent with calling me to tie up my evenings and leaving me hanging. His excuses for not showing up were never elaborate which left little room for interrogation. I managed to keep my cool during this time because I was not his girlfriend. He didn't have to answer to me but I was still working on that. The funny thing about this situation is when he was with me, he was with me wholeheartedly. I had his undivided attention and it was intense. I believe this is what made his undesirable behavior tolerable. So, in an effort to keep the ball rolling and maintain my cool, I wrote to him. I spoke to him in No Worries, Just Concerns.

Patience

Patience
Today, tomorrow and the next day
let's say we'll stay growing
Even if it rains
Baby and if it pours
my umbrella's big enough for yours…
And all that space that you needed
I greet it now
I meet it at the threshold
that flesh hold I had on you
was kind of getting old
I know it
Although you tried not to show it
I commend you for making it seem
effortless.
the rest of this spoken word
is meant to speak life into us
I'm fighting for us
cause I never knew love like this before
I want to explore every crease and crevice
let this new light
take me to a new height of my
Patience
today, tomorrow and the next day
Just say we'll stay growing
Even if it rains
baby and if it pours
my umbrella's big enough for your struggles
I struggle too
But I could feed off your bright energy

and breed a synergy
that's admirable
like the Will's and Jada's
And let the haters that love to hate
learn to take heed to the power of a black couple on the rise!
I got a prize and I recognize
your potential.
I'm not asleep
But a weak woman would have dozed off
rolled off the bed
and cracked her head on the nightstand
woke up looking for the right man
when he was resting on her left...
tired from a long day's work.
Patience
is a virtue and umm...
I've learned from the
woman in Proverbs 31
I'm using my strongest muscle
so the struggle is minute
in this pursuit of happiness
that's not diluted
but rooted in tangible admiration
adding the duration
of this relationship
will be having people taking sips
of whatever it was we used
to get us here so abruptly.
so don't interrupt
the flow
although the physical is moving slow
my emotions are on a rollercoaster ride

Don't stop
Don't stop…

Elucidation

Okay. There is a lot going on here. I was still dealing with Quincy. I believe this was the last draw for me. Going through this piece I was fighting to hold on to something I wanted but did not have: a man and love. It was said so beautifully. After rereading it, I almost believe it myself. This piece was written out of total desperation. I wanted to believe the stories he was telling me were true. He was having it hard. He was settling into a new job. He was having some issues with his children and his ex-wife. His child support had gone up. You name it. I had heard every alibi under the sun. With that being said, I made up my mind that I was going to be patient and let him know that I am here for the long haul. I wanted to remind him that his struggles didn't have to be carried alone. I thought I was painting a picture of the strong black woman. But I was confused and had it all wrong. What I was really doing was giving in to my fears of being alone. I was showing myself weak to this man and he was fully aware. I noticed that I was willing to overlook the subtleties when it was convenient. Wanting a man, being lonely, horny, or needing financial assistance all caused me to weaken my integrity. Lucky for me, I have girlfriends who love and care for me enough to show me things when I can't see them on my own. They told me often that something seemed fishy about this man. They couldn't see what I had seen. Because of this, I was able to pull it together before permanent damage was done. I never shared this poem with him or anyone else. He and I made the time to have a serious talk and made the decision to gracefully part ways.

Waiting on You

This love thing can be so hard
on guard and off guard
it's taxing on my soul
I feel I've damn near lost control
feeling the heat of desperation
because the frustration of finding
a strong, black, honorable man
is finally taking its toll.
Confused on what to do next
considering dressing scantily
and settling for empty sex.
but I am simply not that far gone yet.
knowing that the white man
is not the right man
but because he is available he can be
tonight's man
isn't quite my plan
but I find myself gazing in that direction.
seeking security and some sense of protection.
but who am I kidding.
what white man wouldn't be willing to
lay down with an exotic black women?
Well, I'm still waiting on my honorable strong black man
Please tell me you're coming.

Elucidation

After all of my searching I still had not found my mate. I was becoming numb. All of these thoughts crossed my mind on numerous occasions. Some I had the opportunity to carry out; others I did not, which was probably for my own good. Most of the time I try not to include others in my mess, but I have to speak of black women as a whole when I say this. We are hungry for decent black men and because there seem to be less to go around, we force ourselves to be content with something different. We sacrifice swag for security. Substitute a night in laying it down for a night out on the town. Did you get that? I think what men need to realize when they cross paths with women who are behaving in some of the ways that I addressed in the poem, is that they may be missing a vital part of their existence. The part that understands their needs from the inside out...**God**, who is all knowing and will recognize their need for the strong honorable black man.

Remember Me?

I am sick of being called
Bitch.
I am your mother
wife
daughter
sister
cousin
niece
and aunt.
More than a piece of ass whenever you want.
Why do you degrade me
more than any other?
You are my father
my husband
my uncle
my brother.
Are you not the chief model of
how Black Queens should be treated?
If we are not loved and protected by you,
are we all not defeated?
Remember me black man.
we built this land together.
Remember yourself
Separation was the plan
After division comes death

Elucidation

Remember me? Remember us? Remember your rib? This is for you black man. Black women need to know that you respect us. We need to know that you give a damn about our future and the futures of our children. Keep in mind that I didn't say your children or my children. I said our children! Shouldn't you be the head of this campaign? Showing our boys how to love and raise their families with honor rather than slander. Giving our girls an example of how black women should be treated in public and behind closed doors. Are we so far behind that we still have not learned to love ourselves enough to take care of us? To protect us? No black man, the weight of this race is not solely on your shoulders. But whether you have a platform that reaches one or millions, you are in a position to produce change. It starts with one. Can someone make a big deal out of remembering the statute from which we came and build on that? We cannot remain as we are. Black men and women cannot survive divided.

Aspiration

I've done it again
I've won it again
That fire and desire of
a love brand new
still in the cocoon
yet waiting to bloom
in its due season.
He's given me reason
to set aside my apprehensions.
To look forward to the ascension of this union
and the need to mention that he knows
what he's doing with his tongue.
I've already begun to go crazy
with hopes that maybe he'll
come and go with me.
Slow with me.
Slow walks
added to the that slow talk we had last night
and if I might
add a few words of encouragement.
Nourishment is necessary for this thing to flourish
I hope he's taking notes.
Totes images of me
and my body art on the right side of his brain
While the left is trying to maintain his
upward expression.
That sign that in record time I've left an impression.
As he did.
And he did leave me wanting.
Taunting me with his lips.

I'm still trying to come to grips
with the fact that he can move me without so much as a touch.
Who knew that his words could do so much.
He's super and
only a super man
can play with the hand being dealt
no matter how many times you shuffle
the power between us is felt
Deep…Undeniable
The idea of you and I is viable
don't deny me the privilege of knowing you
well beneath the surface image
and don't mistake this game for a scrimmage
I'm playing to win it
with the desire to open wide
and guide you in it.
I'm guessing
this is a blessing undisguised
and we will become each others
prized possessions
even in the least
we'd be each others greatest lesson.
To question it would be saying
God was wrong
And I know you don't want to sing that song.
Drown in me
Down me like your favorite drink
and enjoy the process
of reaching that high that I'm sure to give
LIVE…

Elucidation

He laughed with me. He held me. He kissed me. He spoke to me with his caresses. He respected me. He left me wanting more. In one evening this man changed my life. He made me go against what I had believed to be true about my wants and needs. I didn't really know what I wanted until I found him. What I desired before was no more because I now desired him. What I needed before was void because I now needed him. It all became ever so clear. This man here was the one.

MILESTONE

Tomorrow is the day for the labor of the lazy.
I must act now!

For My Husband

Dear Christopher,

I am in complete awe when I think of you. Sometimes I just look at you and smile because I can't think of any words to express the emotion dwelling in me. I listen to you. You speak to me with your actions, your eyes, and your embrace. I have been learning you since the day we met. In our very first conversation you were funny, inquisitive and slightly reserved. I liked it. You drew me in even when I had made a conscious decision to walk away from what I had created you to be in my mind. I listened to how you spoke to your children. Paid close attention to their responses to you. I watched how you handled your cousin's passing. I admired how you turned down the opportunity to spend time with me doing something you hadn't done before, to spend time with your cousin in her final days. How even in your grieving you managed to make the time to send a text just to say hello to little ol' me whom you hadn't known for more than a week. And finally, when we had the chance to come together and spend a significant amount of time with each other, you allowed yourself to let go....to feel. The look in your eyes is one that I will never forget. I recognize it every time I see even a glimpse of it. I hunger for you when you are away. I couldn't understand for a while how your presence in my life could demand so much of me. I am involuntarily driven to do things that are specifically designed for you. The person I am to you I am not to anyone else. I am who I am to you because of who you are to me. Is this making any sense?

I have been trying not to say this. I've been fighting to hold on just a little longer. But my body, my heart, my mind would not allow me to wait another day. It's funny how we force ourselves to wait on things like this. We are always in a hurry when it comes to things that are meaningless and have no real significance in life. Oh but this…this is something we all force ourselves to wait on even when we KNOW! My physical being is relieved as I type these words. I had to give birth to this today.

I remember telling you about my brother briefly. Just so you could be aware of some of the things I was dealing with outside of you. Days later we had lunch. You reached for my hand to bless our food and you took the time to pray for my brother as well. How could you have been so thoughtful? My heart must have skipped a beat. You cared enough about me to consider him. You were and are my SUNSHINE on a cloudy day. When I send you those text messages they are not sent haphazardly.

When you kiss me….Oh when you kiss me I get chills throughout my body. You take my breath away in the most intimate way possible. When you hold me I feel secure. I feel sure of us. I feel sure of this.

Last night I said "guess what?" and didn't follow through. At first I didn't want to say it. I didn't want to be the first. It seems silly now. But then (as I thought about it more) I didn't want to just say it. I wanted to be able to tell you why in detail. I wanted you to have a thorough understanding of how or why I feel the way that I do. I didn't want to be interrupted. I wanted you to have it in print. I wanted you to be able to look back and remember everything I said to you word for word. Our children may read this one day and they will know how much I love you. I have fallen completely head over heels in love with you Christopher Dennis. I'm so glad I could say it out loud. I'm thinking it constantly. I feel it constantly. So now you know…

Guess what? Ha ha ha…..there it is, baby!

I Love You Too

Well hello to you. It is crazy to hear how you feel about things. I always feel I talk so much and go on and on that I don't give you a chance to say your thoughts all the time. I am so happy that you wrote that for me. I knew that's what you were going to say yesterday that's why I said I already know and me too. A few weeks ago when I said guess what and said never mind, that's what I was feeling. I know that making that declaration is important, scary, and kind of weird. It makes you uncomfortable being on either end of it. But when I looked at you that first night I was in love already. In those few moments that it took to let myself go into another feeling from the sorrow I felt from losing someone so close to me. I never felt pain as deep as I did when I lost my cousin; I learned that that kind of love comes with so much joy and memories. So each day I tried to show her that I loved her as my cousin, my sister, my friend, my hero, I began to know how much love I had in my heart. I know that I don't want to die without being able to share that love with someone who is worthy of it, and I don't want to die without someone being able to share that kind of love with me. Even to this moment I am not sure if there is a jar that can fit all of the love I wish to share with you. So when I look in your eyes I just go away into happiness. I am able to see all I have been through and see where I want to go and see you there with me. It feels real good. So when I look at you I love you, and when I kiss you I love you, and when you laugh I love you. When you look back at me I love you more, and when you kiss me back I love you more, and when I laugh at you I love you more. I love you so much that I am shy around you. I am confident around you, and vulnerable around you. It's so unknown and scary about how our future will develop that it excites me to think about it and plan it. I want to find a good church for us because I want to do right by our relationship and be able to qualify to be your man because right now I want to be better and do more. That's just how I am. But I'll get there. I hope you felt the love I have for you on many days and I hope I can make up for the difference if on some days you don't feel it because I mean only but well. But baby I love you back, I love you too.

I was speechless

Certainty

How many ways can I say...
What I meant to say was I can't get enough of you
I've fallen out of lust with you
and it's starting to feel like love with you
or something close to it
somehow I knew it from the start
that I'd give you my heart
it wasn't a fallacy
or said haphazardly that night at the bar
when I said you'd marry me
I spoke it into existence
and told all your boys so that two years from now
we both have a witness
regarding what I thought of you.
what I saw in the heart of you was pure
How many ways can I say...
I'm sure

MILESTONE

The best way to get over a man
is to get on top of another.
I was an idiot!

Revenge

Revenge
Is it a means to an end?
Or a means to a friend
that's really not a friend
but a sin that's lying in wait?
Waiting on a sign
that my ish is out of line
So it can be there in my time
of discomfort.
Easing me.
Stroking my ego
To the point where I am no longer asking
"Where did he go?"
See, we go way back
Revenge and I...
Back in the days
When I use to wear braids,
Revenge sported waves.
Kept me dazed on most occasions
But I always came out with light abrasions.
And that was alright with me.
It was a small price to pay to heal a wound so deep.
But whether it was deep, shallow, solid or hollow
Recognizing that gut feeling is a hard thing to swallow
Especially when I want to ignore it.
Store it deep
So that when I'm around my peeps
Signs of my distress don't seep.
Cause I'm sophisticated and I'm chic
And totally unaware that they can see that I'm weak

Like a crackhead
Walking round town thinking she cute
I'm talking circles around my situation
to prove that I'm astute.
"Can't nobody pull the wool over my eyes"
Surprise!
I didn't even see it coming.
Now I'm wondering.
Should I be running for Revenge?
Knowing that it's not a means to an end
But a means to a friend
That's really not a friend
But a sin that lying in wait?
Consequences...
Now I gotta add this man to my list of pretenses!

Elucidation

For a long time, revenge was how I handled my problems with others. I always felt the best way to make myself feel better was to retaliate. When I grew into my womanhood I learned that it was better to just let go and move on. When I wrote this piece I was in a place where I thought about going back to my old ways. My boyfriend at the time was not answering his cell phone. I was calling him like a madwoman. For him, this was abnormal behavior. He usually answers on the first couple of rings or he'd call me back immediately. Hours had gone by. Time was getting the best of me and I was getting the idea that maybe I should call someone who will answer the phone since he was soooo busy! In that same instant, I thought of the consequences my actions might lead to and how that would damage my integrity if he found out. So instead of doing something silly, I put my thoughts in my poetry.

I'm Coming

Hey you!
I was hoping I could see you tonight.
He was like…
"I'm coming"
And like a thief in the night he came
Framed me with his attention
And with every extension
he loved me hard.
My guard had dissolved
as he solved every single problem
I had created from past anxieties.
The fight in me wanted to remain cautious
But this Boss just made me relax
Tried to give me my space
But I was like…
Come back.
He said…
"I'm coming"
And like a thief in the night he came
Tamed me
Named me his wife
Then gave it to me like he was
Recreating life
I didn't wanna stop it
Cause he was in the pocket
Can we prolong it for a minute B?
I'm not ready for it to be a memory.
He was like…
"I'm coming"
And like a thief in the night he came

Rained on me
but it was like rain in the summertime
I was trying to watch the sky
But was blinded by the shine
So all I could really do is close my eyes
And feel
My goodness I was thrilled
No raincoat required
When I received the weather report
I was wired to explore what Mother Nature
Had in store for me
I was hoping there was a little more for me
When he whispered
"I'm coming"
And like a thief in the night he came
Can I blame him?
Yes!
Cause I'm giving him my Yes
My Yes Yes
And My Yes Lords
Hitting high notes with
dry vocal cords
I was thirsty
But while he was working me
All I could think was...
"Can I have another drink?"
Cause...
I'm just not getting my fill
So if you will...
I'd love to go one or two more rounds,
and with every one of his 170 pounds
He was like...

"I'm coming"
And like a thief in the night he came.
I came
We came together
Like never before
Our love rang louder
Than a lion's roar
Louder than a fan
Praising his final four
Louder than a crowd
when Kobe hit that three for the final score.
Need I say more?
Yes!
See
cause
He blessed me
He was
More than a conqueror
He was as stallion
Cause at the last mile's end...
He kept going
He kept going
He kept growing
This was getting heavy
Cause I wasn't ready
For this to be continued
I read the menu
And I've already had every single dish
He was like
"You coming?"
I was like
"I wish"

I wish I was able
But my body's growing numb and
Will soon be disabled
Can I have a few more moments to become stable?
I'm confused
Yet highly amused by his tenacity
And still he kept asking me
questions like
"You coming?"
All I could do was stutter
Like umm…
Can I have a piece of gum?
Or something to avoid this cotton mouth
It's hot in this house
Can we open a window?
Then his voiced started to crescendo
With every innuendo
Like…
"This is what u wanted, right?"
Right
"This is how u wanted it, right?"
Right
Soon after he caressed me
He left me
There to
Wallow in my sweat
Regret was farfetched
I was tingling
Doorbell ringing
But I wasn't up for mingling
I was thinking on how I
Wanted to do it again

That's when I decided to phone in
I was hoping I could see you tonight.
Or something…
He was like…
"I'm coming"

I'm Coming

The aftermath

Like a thief in the night he came
But it wasn't the same
He
Seemed so disconnected
Like there was a lack of respect
It was awkward to be around him
Just days before I was happy to have found him
Happy to just be
Holding him
Molding our bodies together like we were meant…
Even though I meant
To wait to become one with him
I didn't want my journey to be done with him
I didn't only want to come with him
I wanted to go
But like a thief in the night he came
to rob me of my soul.

Elucidation

The ability to share mind, body, life, and love with someone else is the key to living. It's how we as human beings evolve. But in order to experience the fullness of what that is like we have to do it God's way. It was His original plan for man not to be alone and we women were never alone (*Genesis Chapter 2 Verse 18*). See, when Eve was pulled out of Adam she didn't know what being alone felt like. She had never experienced not having Adam (*Genesis Chapter 2 Verses 21-24*). This is part of the reason why women today do foolish things to keep a man around. We came into the world with one! Because of the introduction of sin, our entire reason for being here is thrown off course (*Genesis Chapter 3 Verses 1-19*). Women are out hunting for men and husbands before seeking God. Men are out looking for Jezebels instead of allowing God to lead them to their wives and we have been tricked into believing that fulfilling fleshly desires are reason enough to go against His word (*Proverbs Chapter 5 Verses 1-23*). So we dress to seduce. We give in to their sexual desires. Some of us neglect our children who would probably not be here if we had followed God's plan in the first place (*Proverbs 31 Verses 10-31*). We have done everything under the sun to entice them when subconsciously all we really want to do is get back to what is natural to us. Get back to God's original will for us. Don't think for one second that Satan isn't well aware of this. He didn't even have to come like a thief in the night. He looked me dead in the face. And because I was spiritually weak…I came.

MILESTONE

You know you have found love
when you just can't seem to put it into words.

Boomerang

Just like a seesaw
What goes up must come down
A boomerang lost will soon be found
Sounds adolescent doesn't it?
But it wasn't it
Was grown but not sexy
Uncomplicated
But complex see
This boomerang was laced
Graced with multi-blade ends
So the beauty of it can be seen in the wind
Sharpened to pierce seamlessly
So it's easy to mend
Bend
Back into shape
Jiggle, not shake up a situation
But merely fall back into normal rotation
That's if...
Its journey was a success.
But it wasn't
It was what is was
And it was a mess.
This boomerang was tossed
Caught
And pierced someone's chest
See through!
Busted a "C"
A "U"
Then busted a left
Need I remind you...

This was supposed to go right!
Right?
With my right eye
I winked with a tight eye
And turned my back....
Now guess where the boomerang is at.
Crying
It kinda feels like I'm dying
Can't deny that I made it
Thinking this can't be something I have created.
The maker of my own destiny.
Not realizing the pain I was prepping for
was really meant for me.
Meant to be?
Maybe.
But to do it all again you couldn't even pay me.
although it made me a better woman.
for next time I'll see temptation
when it's coming.
Now I'm
hung by a jury
made of my only love's fury
Guilty
As proven
Does this mean that my integrity
Is ruined?
NO.
I have been challenged to change
Given the opportunity to use
my heart in conjunction with my brain
Maintain this in which we've built
The chance to live beyond the guilt

I've been blessed in what came as only
hurt to me.
the measure of this man
was seen in how he handled himself
in adversity.
He is of more worth to me
Than he can ever know
But he will be the first to see
Cause all I can do now is SHOW.

Elucidation

I cheated with unintentional intentions. I was caught and the ramifications were intense. He forgave me. I have been a far better person ever since.

Change

Change
Whether it's accepted
Or neglected
It is to be expected.
Unavoidable newness
If I had a choice
Would I really want to do this?
Change
Rearrange my life to fit this new me.
Rest in it
Only pour my best in it
And find comfort in this cycle of spring.
Or leave my king open in a wild game of chess
Checkmate.

MILESTONE

I have always known that I had the power

to write my own destiny,

The gotcha is...I just learned how to pick up a pen!

I've Been Paying Attention

I've been paying attention
Even when I fail to mention
You
Working hard daily
Trying to make way for the babies
Dividing your time for the ladies in your vision
I've been paying attention
Watching you grow stronger
Thinking…
If I look away for a second longer
I may miss something outrageous
Stages
From a man
To a man's man
To a man who stands through almost any test
A man who works even when he needs rest
And at best
A man who'll give till his very last breath
Yet
Would give that too if he had nothing left.
Oh!
I've been paying attention to your woes
Paying no mind to those who help you not
Somehow you manage to work with what you've got
So today this something you don't have to mention
As a lady in your vision
I've made the decision
To help more with the kids

And give you your way
For one hour every day
Will be fathers' day!

MILESTONE

I will keep things around me that make me smile.
I am beautiful when I am smiling.

Emotions
A Journal Entry

January 11, 2002
8:32 p.m.

I'm happy
Excited
Anxious
Scared
Sad
Heartbroken
Fed up
Relieved
Disappointed
Drained
Overjoyed
Confused...
Open
Refreshed
Strong
Weak
a hopeless romantic
Creative
Spontaneous
Crazy
I love to love and be loved
Cry when I'm hurt
Smile because I want to
And if it was totally up to me...I'd never ever stop!

Patience
A Journal Entry

Patient
Be patient
Patience told me to be still.
Patience told me not to rush time
Because I won't get there any faster than time will allow.
Then I said to patience, "I don't know how!"
She said, "Do what you can with the time that you have."
I said, "There is not enough time."
Patience looked at me and laughed!

Slow Rain

Life gives you time
to think and rethink and act
or take action
I've made the decision to
to take this position and
act like a woman in love.
A woman above the naysayers
because they live life in layers
of disappointment and fear.
Not I
Not this year
This tear you see welling
up in my eye is not
caused by pain.
But by the slow rain of
that oomph that I had not
known till now
I feel now
that I can till this garden forever
With all the clever
ways that it makes my flowers bloom
and constantly making room to grow more
I know more of that slow rain is yet to come
Shower me!

Final thoughts

The things I have experienced in my short lifetime I would wish on no one. I have learned from every experience good, bad, and ugly. I have loved and lost. I have given up my body and my will. I have sacrificed my integrity for moments of pleasure that ended in regret. Oh yes, I have done some crazy things because of a man. Looking back, I found that this is the common thread in most of my journey.

What God has revealed to me is that all of these things could have been avoided if I had put Him first. Had I been concerned with what God wanted for my life, I would have been able to fight temptation. I would have been able to see all the traps that Satan was trying to get me caught up with. When I was living in and being led by my flesh, he knew just what to do to keep me there. He was sly. He catered to my fleshly desires and I eagerly obliged because I was blind. Satan was able to use one of God's greatest gifts against me because I didn't have enough of God's word to stand on. I thought I was sowing my oats and experiencing life before settling down, but my foundation was weak; so was I. *Luke Chapter 6 Verses 46-49*

I was put through the wringer for many years thanks to my lack of wisdom and understanding of God's word. It didn't happen overnight, but I found that knowing the word isn't enough. I had to become proactive. I had to be a doer of His word in order for it to be affective in my life (Ecclesiastes Chapter 12 Verse 13-14). I can't help but wonder what my life would be like had I known this years ago? Had I had my heart and ears inclined enough to hear Him. Although there may have been a lot of tough roads less traveled, I would not be here today sharing my experiences and growth with all of you.

My wish is that my path can help someone change their mind about taking the same route. To be a guide for those who have already done so and don't know how to turn around or don't believe they can. To show women that all of that pain, fear, shame, confusion, disappointment, lack of self worth, and past hurts that we bury deep down in our bellies, can sometimes make us prisoners to ourselves. Understand that we must let go and let God do what he must to help us through the healing process. Our struggles are not in vain for they can be used for His glory (Mathew 26 Verse 42).

God bless you.